Headway

5th edition

Pre-intermediate Workbook without key

Liz & John Soars • Jo McCaul

Contents

1 Getting to know you → page 6

Grammar
Tense revision – present, past and future 6
Questions 7
Question words 8

Vocabulary
Right word, wrong word 10

Everyday English
Social expressions 11

REVIEW 11

2 Let's get together → page 12

Grammar
Present Simple 12
have and *have got* 13
Present Simple and Continuous 14

Vocabulary
Things I like doing 16

Everyday English
Making conversation 17

REVIEW 17

3 Good news, bad news → page 18

Grammar
Past Simple 18
Past Continuous 19
Past Simple and Continuous 20

Vocabulary
Adverbs 22
have + noun 22

Everyday English
Saying when 23

REVIEW 23

4 Food for thought → page 24

Grammar
Countable and uncountable nouns 24
Expressions of quantity 25
Pronouns – *something/no one …* 26
Articles – *a/an, the* or –? 26

Vocabulary
A piece of cake 28
Shops 28
Food 28

Everyday English
Can you come for dinner? 29

REVIEW 29

Stop and check   Units 1–4 → page 30

5 The future's in your hands → page 32

Grammar
Verb patterns 32
Future forms 34

Vocabulary
Phrasal verbs 36
The verb *get* 36

Everyday English
Expressing doubt and certainty 37

REVIEW 37

6 History repeats itself → page 38

Grammar
Present Perfect 38
never, already, just, yet 39
for, since and *ago* 39
Present Perfect and Past Simple 40

Vocabulary
Word endings 42

Everyday English
Agree with me! 43

REVIEW 43

7 Simply the best → page 44

Grammar
What's it like?	44
Comparing two people	45
Superlatives	46
Prepositions	46
Comparatives and superlatives	46

Vocabulary
Synonyms and antonyms	48

Everyday English
What's on?	49

REVIEW — 49

8 Living dangerously → page 50

Grammar
have to	50
must	51
should	52

Vocabulary
Not a thing to wear!	54

Everyday English
At the doctor's	55

REVIEW — 55

Stop and check   Units 5–8 → page 56

9 What a story! → page 58

Grammar
Past Perfect and Past Simple	58
Conjunctions	60

Vocabulary
Feelings	62
Homonyms	62

Everyday English
Exclamations with *so* and *such*	63

REVIEW — 63

10 All-time greats → page 64

Grammar
Passives	64
Active or passive?	66
Past participles as adjectives	66

Vocabulary
Compound nouns	68
Adverb + adjective	68

Everyday English
On the phone	69

REVIEW — 69

11 People with a passion → page 70

Grammar
Present Perfect Simple and Continuous	70
Present Perfect Continuous	71
Present Perfect Simple or Continuous?	71
Tense review	72

Vocabulary
Stages of life	74

Everyday English
Finding the right words	74

REVIEW — 75

12 You never know … → page 76

Grammar
First Conditional	76
Second Conditional	77
First or Second Conditional?	78
might	78

Vocabulary
bring and *take*, *come* and *go*	80
Prepositions	80

Everyday English
Thank you and goodbye!	81

REVIEW — 81

Stop and check   Units 9–12 → page 82

Irregular verbs → page 84

Phonetic symbols → page 85

Course overview

5th edition
Headway

Welcome to **Headway 5th edition**. Here's how the blended syllabus helps you link learning in the classroom with meaningful practice outside.

Student's Book

All the language and skills you need to improve your English, with grammar, vocabulary and skills work in every unit. Also available as an e-book.

Use your Student's Book in class with your teacher.

Workbook

Exclusive practice to match your Student's Book, unit by unit.

Use your Workbook for homework or for self-study to give you new input and practice.

ACTIVITIES   AUDIO   VIDEO   WORDLISTS

AT HOME

Go to **headwayonline.com** and use your code on your Access Card to log into the Online Practice.

LOOK AGAIN
- Review the language from every lesson
- Watch the videos and listen to all the class audio again

PRACTICE
- Develop your skills with extra Reading, Writing, Listening and Speaking practice

CHECK YOUR PROGRESS
- Test yourself on the main language from the unit and get instant feedback
- Try an extra challenge

Online Practice

Look again at Student's Book language you want to review or that you missed in class, do extra ***Practice*** activities, and ***Check your Progress*** on what you've learnt so far.

Use the Online Practice at home to extend your learning and get instant feedback on your progress.

headwayonline.com

Course overview 5

1 Getting to know you

- Tense revision – present, past and future
- Questions
- Question words
- Right word, wrong word
- Social expressions

Grammar
Tense revision – present, past and future

1 Complete the texts with the verb forms in the box.

Johanna Becker
from the US

| has   speaks   'm studying   'm hoping   don't want   was   moved   studied   ~~was born~~ |

Johanna Becker is a student. She [1] *was born* in Germany, but she [2] _____ to Boston in the US with her parents when she [3] _____ just six years old. She [4] _____ two older brothers. She [5] _____ three languages – German, English, and Spanish.

'I [6] _____ law at Stanford University from 2014 to 2017, but I [7] _____ to become a lawyer. Now I [8] _____ anthropology at Oxford University. After that, I [9] _____ to get a job in Mexico. I really want to work at the Museum of Anthropology in Mexico City.'

Garlen Bernard
from France

| comes   like   found   takes   play   don't like   missed   'm living   's teaching   made   teaches   'm going to look |

Garlen is a teacher. He [1] _____ from France. He normally [2] _____ mathematics at the Sorbonne, but at the moment he [3] _____ mathematics at McGill University in Montreal for a year.

'I [4] _____ living in Canada very much, the people are warm and friendly. At first, I [5] _____ home a lot, but I soon [6] _____ friends and [7] _____ an apartment. I [8] _____ in an apartment with three other teachers – it's fun. I [9] _____ living on my own. It only [10] _____ me five minutes to walk downtown, where I can shop or go to cafés and clubs. I often [11] _____ sports here – football and tennis. I [12] _____ for a permanent job in Canada when I finish my year at McGill University. Maybe here in Montreal? Who knows? I really like Vancouver, too.'

Anna and Don
from England

| have   love   's teaching   's helping   're staying   're doing   didn't want   graduated   decided   're going to train |

Anna and Don are from Exeter in England. They both [1] _____ last year, but they [2] _____ to start their careers immediately, so they [3] _____ to live and work abroad for a year. At the moment, they [4] _____ volunteer work in Kenya. They [5] _____ at Camp Kenya with 50 other volunteers from all over the world. They're both working in the local community: Anna [6] _____ English, and Don [7] _____ the local people to build schools and playgrounds. 'The kids [8] _____ playing football,' says Don, 'and now they [9] _____ a real pitch to play on.'

When Anna and Don go back to England, they [10] _____ to be teachers.

Forming the tense

2 Put the verbs into the correct tense and form (positive or negative).

1 Johanna **wasn't born** (*born*) in the US.
2 She _____ (*speak*) Portuguese.
3 In the photo, Johanna _____ (*carry*) some books.
4 Garlen _____ (*be*) French.
5 At the moment he _____ (*live*) with three other teachers.
6 Garlen _____ (*like*) living on his own.
7 Anna and Don _____ (*live*) in England at the moment.
8 They _____ (*finish*) university last year.
9 When they go back to England, they _____ _____ (*train*) to be teachers.

3 Choose the correct form of the verb.

1 She's very clever. She ___ three languages.
   a 's speaking   b speak   c speaks

2 'Would you like a cigarette?'
   'No, thanks. I ___.'
   a don't smoke   b no smoke   c 'm not smoking

3 I ___ to the cinema yesterday evening.
   a go   b was   c went

4 Where ___ in Argentina?
   a you stayed   b did you stay   c you stay

5 My weekend was very boring. I ___ anything.
   a didn't do   b didn't   c not do

6 This is a great party! Everyone ___ a good time.
   a has   b having   c 's having

7 'What ___ tonight?'
   'I'm going out with friends.'
   a are you doing   b you do   c do you do

8 I don't know this word. What ___?
   a does it mean   b means it   c does mean

9 Next year I ___ study at university.
   a go to   b 'm going to   c going to

Questions

4 Complete the questions.

1 'What kind of cake *is* he *going to make*?'
  'He's going to make a chocolate cake.'
2 'What _____ Zoe _____?'
  'She's playing on her iPad in her room.'
3 'Where _____ Jane and Peter _____?'
  'They live in a flat, in north London.'
4 '_____ Jane _____ a car?'
  'No, she doesn't.'
5 'Where _____ you _____ on holiday?'
  'I'm going to Italy.'
6 'What _____ you _____ last night?'
  'I watched the football.'
7 'Where _____ your grandmother born?'
  'She was born in Stockholm.'
8 'When _____ she get _____?'
  'She got married in 1980.'

🔊 **1.1** Listen and check.

Auxiliaries

5 Put the words on the right in the correct place in the questions.

1	Where ⋀ Maria come from? *does*	does
2	What language she speaking now?	is
3	What you doing tonight?	are
4	Where you buy your jeans?	did
5	What you going to cook for dinner?	are
6	How much money he have?	does
7	You go to work yesterday?	did
8	What your father do?	does

Question words

6 Complete the conversation with question words.

Mum Morning, Tom. ¹ *How* are you this morning?
Tom Morning, Mum. Fine, thanks. I'm just a bit tired.
Mum I didn't hear you come home last night.
² _____ time did you get in?
Tom Not that late. About 11.00.
Mum ³ _____ did you go?
Tom Just round to Alex's house. We played cards.
Mum Sounds like fun. [*beep*] Tom, was that your phone?
Tom Yeah. Oh!
Mum ⁴ _____'s the matter?
Tom Nothing. It's a text from Lucia.
Mum ⁵ _____'s Lucia?
Tom She's a girl I met on holiday in Spain.
Mum Really? What does she want?
Tom She's coming to Oxford.
Mum ⁶ _____ is she coming?
Tom Because she's going to learn English.
Mum ⁷ _____ school is she going to?
Tom She doesn't know yet. She wants my advice.
Mum There are lots of good schools in Oxford.
⁸ _____'s she coming?
Tom Next month.
Mum Well, ⁹ _____ don't you invite her for dinner when she's here?
Tom OK. I'll ask her. Thanks, Mum.

1.2 Listen and check.

7 Match a question in **A** with an answer in **B**.

A
1 What do you do?
2 Who did you go out with?
3 Where do you live?
4 When's your birthday?
5 Why are you wearing a suit?
6 How many bedrooms are there?
7 How much did you pay for it?
8 How are you?
9 Whose phone is this?
10 Which phone network do you use?

B		
a	☐	£45.
b	☐	Three.
c	☐	Fine, thanks. And you?
d	☐	My friend Alex.
e	☒ 1	I'm a teacher.
f	☐	Vodafone.
g	☐	April 22nd.
h	☐	It's mine. Thanks.
i	☐	In a flat in the centre of town.
j	☐	I'm going to a friend's wedding.

1.3 Listen and check.

who's or *whose*?

8 Complete the sentences with *who's* or *whose*.

1 '_____ going to the cinema on Saturday?'
'Everyone except George.'

2 '_____ is that beautiful coat?'
'It's Olivia's. It cost nearly £400!'

3 '_____ bag is this?'
'It's mine.'

4 '_____ that ringing at the door?'
'No idea, I'll go and see.'

5 '_____ that handsome boy with Sue?'
'It's Jim. He's her younger brother.'

6 'Do you know _____ house that is?'
'Yes, Mr Jones lives there.'

Best friends and brilliant athletes

9 Read about **Menna Fitzpatrick**, a Paralympic ski racer, and her guide, **Jen Kehoe**. Write the headings in the correct place in the text.

Ears become eyes	Friends forever
A friend and guide	It came good in the end
Thanks to her parents	

10 Complete the questions about Menna and Jen.

1 'How many medals _did_ they _win_?'
  'Four.'
2 'When _____ Menna _____ skiing?'
  'When she was five.'
3 'Why _____ the crowds _____ silent at competitions?'
  'So that the skier can hear instructions.'
4 'What _____ Jen _____?'
  'She's an army officer.'
5 '_____ Menna and Jen _____ best friends immediately?'
  'Yes, they did.'
6 '_____ the girls _____ their first race at the Games?'
  'No, they didn't. They crashed out.'
7 'Why _____ Jen proud?'
  'Because they won gold.'
8 '_____ they _____ _____ continue to ski together?'
  'Yes, they are. And they're hoping for more success.'

11 Complete the sentences with one word each time.

1 Menna's parents _____ her to feel the same as her sisters.
2 Menna _____ an only child, she _____ two older sisters.
3 Her father sometimes _____ remember that she was behind him.
4 Menna _____ to her guide carefully when she's skiing.
5 Jen _____ Menna's guide in 2015.
6 The UK _____ just one gold medal in South Korea.
7 The girls are _____ to be friends forever.

Menna and Jen – *Paralympic skiers*

Menna Fitzpatrick and Jennifer Kehoe are the most successful Paralympians ever, and they're best friends. They won four medals, including a gold, at the 2018 Paralympics in South Korea. What is the secret of their incredible success?

1 _____

Menna was born with less than 5% vision, but her parents didn't want her to feel different to other children. She did the same sports as her older sisters and started skiing when she was only five years old. She followed her father down the slopes. Sometimes he forgot Menna was behind him and he took her down difficult slopes and even off-piste*! She was clearly a 'natural'. In 2010 a ski coach noticed her and she started training with the British Parasnowsport team.

2 _____

Skiing at 110 kph is not easy even when you can see clearly – but imagine skiing with less than 5% vision. Menna says that it's like skiing in thick fog. Your eyes can't see, so your ears are everything – you need to hear what your guide is saying. During competitions, the crowds can't make any noise – they stay completely silent.

3 _____

Jen is an Army Officer in the Royal Engineers. She loved skiing and raced with the Army Ski Team. In 2013, a coach asked her to become a guide for the British Parasnowsport team. She agreed and two years later she was paired with Menna. The two girls immediately became best friends. It was not just the beginning of a friendship, but also a great sporting partnership. They say that they are like sisters who don't fight.

4 _____

In March 2018, at the Winter Paralympic Games in South Korea, the girls crashed out in their opening race. But they didn't give up. They continued to fight and went on to win a bronze and two silver medals. That was good, but then on the final day Menna and Jen won a gold medal – the UK's only gold of the Games! Jen proudly said, 'we fought right to the very end.'

5 _____

Menna and Jen are going to continue skiing together in the future and hope for more success. However, when their skiing partnership does finally end, the girls know that they are going to be friends forever.

off-piste away from the ski tracks

Vocabulary
Right word, wrong word

1 Choose the correct verb for each line.

> play   go

1 Do you want to **play** tennis?
   I **go** ice-skating once a week.

> do   make

2 Good luck in the exam! _____ your best!
   I _____ my own bread every morning.

> say   speak

3 Eduard doesn't _____ English very well.
   I always _____ hello when I see her.

> watch   look

4 Can I _____ at your wedding photos?
   Did you _____ the match last night on TV?

> lend   borrow

5 Can I _____ some money? I'll give it back to you tomorrow.
   Jack is going to _____ us his car for the weekend.

> teach   learn

6 Can you _____ me how to cook? I'm rubbish!
   Do you want to _____ French with me? I'm starting a beginners class next week.

2 <u>Underline</u> two nouns that go with the adjective.

1 delicious   <u>burger</u> / <u>meal</u> / picture
2 interesting   laptop / book / film
3 excited   child / football match / dog
4 strong   coffee / exam / woman
5 funny   man / story / view
6 long   woman / road / story

3 Complete the sentences with the correct preposition.

> in   about   for   at (x2)   to   with   of (x2)   from

1 Look **at** that picture! Isn't it beautiful!
2 I'm waiting _____ the postman to arrive.
3 I'm excited _____ my holiday.
4 Are you good _____ maths?
5 Wikipedia is full _____ useful information.
6 Are you interested _____ politics?
7 You're so right. I totally agree _____ you.
8 The station isn't far _____ here.
9 Can I speak _____ you for a minute?
10 I'm afraid _____ dogs.

4 Complete each pair of sentences with the correct word.

> kind   ~~train~~   left   rest   mean

1 When's the next **train** to London?
   Athletes **train** every day to keep fit.

2 You look tired. You need to _____ more.
   We had lunch and spent the _____ of the day on the beach.

3 What does that _____ in English?
   My uncle is really _____. He never spends any money.

4 A present? For me? How _____ of you!
   What _____ of music do you like?

5 Turn _____ at the end of the street.
   We _____ for the airport at six o'clock in the morning.

10   Unit 1 • Getting to know you

Everyday English
Social expressions

Complete the conversations using one word each time.

1 **A** Thank you so much for your help.
   B You're _welcome_. It was no _____ at all.

2 **A** Hi, Laura. Sorry I'm _____. Bad traffic!
   B That's OK. It doesn't _____. The film doesn't start for another 15 minutes.

3 **A** Can you come to dinner on Saturday?
   B I'm _____, I can't. I'm busy.
   A _____ mind. Perhaps _____ time.

4 **A** Excuse me. _____ you _____ me with this exercise? It's really difficult.
   B Of _____. What don't you understand?
   A All of it!

5 **A** Bye, Stella. _____ a good weekend.
   B Thanks! _____ to you, Ashley. Are you _____ anything nice?
   A Yes. I'm meeting an old school friend _____ dinner on Saturday.
   B Lovely! Have _____!

🔊 1.4 Listen and check.

▶ **Go online** for more skills and language practice.

REVIEW
Grammar

1 Put the words in the correct order.

1 that / bag / is / Whose / green / ?
   _____

2 I / well / exams / didn't / my / do / in
   _____

3 studying / Why / you / English / are / ?
   _____

4 many / How / do / have / children / they / ?
   _____

5 going / visit / in / the / Glasgow / friends / We're / weekend / at / to
   _____

6 Lara / from / Scotland / comes / working / moment / but / she's / at / London / in / the
   _____

7 you / last / get / for / What / birthday / did / your / ?
   _____

8 like / dogs / Martha / doesn't / she's / because / of / scared / them
   _____

Vocabulary

2 Underline the correct word.

1 I want to *go / play* dancing tonight.
2 Marco is mad *of / about* tennis. He plays every week.
3 This is a photo *about / of* my dad when he was young.
4 My journey to work was so *busy / long* this morning. It took two hours!
5 Henry is very clever. He can *say / speak* English, Spanish and Italian.
6 My husband never *makes / does* the housework.
7 I live *in / on* a small two bedroom apartment *with / about* my sister.
8 Nick is very *busy / important*. He studies all day and then works at a restaurant at night.
9 I like Helena's new boyfriend – he's very *interesting / interested*.
10 Can you *learn / teach* me how to ride a bike?

▶ **Go online** to Check your progress.

Unit 1 • Getting to know you   11

2 Let's get together

- Present Simple
- *have* and *have got*
- Present Simple and Continuous
- Things I like doing
- Making conversation

Grammar   Present Simple

Positive, negative and questions

1 Complete the text with the verb forms in the box.

| look | ~~work~~ | wants | do | don't live | works | lives |
| does | have | wears (x2) | | | | |

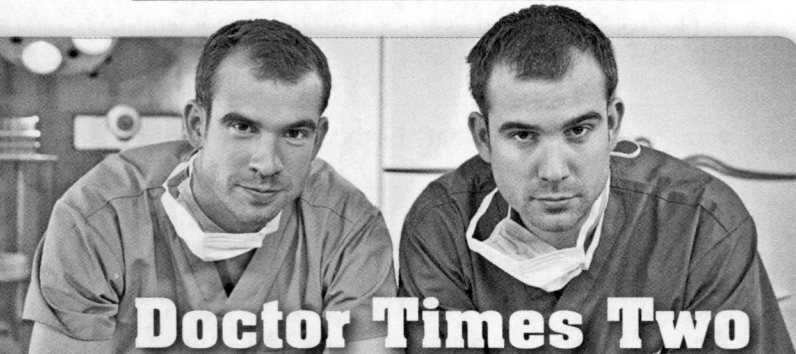

Doctor Times Two

Chris and Xand van Tulleken are identical twins, and they're both doctors. They also ¹ *work* as TV presenters on science programmes and ² _____ a lot of work for charity.

Chris and Xand both ³ _____ medical degrees from Oxford University, and they trained and qualified as doctors at the same hospital. They ⁴ _____ identical, although Chris is taller than Xand by half an inch, and older, too – by seven minutes!

As well as presenting TV shows, Chris is studying at University College London, because he ⁵ _____ to get a PhD. Xand ⁶ _____ in New York and works at Fordham University. He also ⁷ _____ as an editor for the *Oxford Handbook of Humanitarian Medicine* and ⁸ _____ a lot of work for the World Health Organization.

The twins ⁹ _____ in the same country, but they have a common project. They both believe it's very important to get young people interested in science and medicine, and together they present a popular children's medical TV show called *Operation Ouch!*. How can children tell which twin is which on TV? It's easy! Dr Chris always ¹⁰ _____ a blue shirt and Dr Xand ¹¹ _____ a green one!

2 Complete the questions about Chris and Xand.
1 'What *do* Chris and Xand *do*?'
  'They're doctors.'
2 'How much older than Chris _____ Xand?'
  'Seven minutes.'
3 'Where _____ they _____?'
  'Chris lives in the UK and Xand lives in New York.'
4 'Where _____ Xand _____?'
  'At Fordham University.'
5 'What _____ they _____ is important?'
  'To get young people interested in science and medicine.'
6 'Why _____ they _____ different colour shirts on TV?'
  'So the children can tell which twin is which.'

🔊 **2.1** Listen and check.

3 Complete the negative sentences.
1 Chris *doesn't work* (not work) for the *Oxford Handbook of Humanitarian Medicine*.
2 They _____ (not present) a children's talent show.
3 Chris _____ (not live) in New York.
4 They _____ (not wear) the same colour clothes on TV.

4 Write the short answers.
1 'Do Xand and Chris have medical degrees?'
  ' *Yes, they do* .'
2 'Does Chris have a degree from Fordham University?'
  ' _____ .'
3 'Does Xand work for the World Health Organization?'
  ' _____ .'
4 'Do they live in the same country?'
  ' _____ .'

🔊 **2.2** Listen and check.

12   Unit 2 • Let's get together

State verbs

5 Complete the sentences with the verbs in the box in the correct form.

> need   belong   cost   not understand   have
> not know   think   agree   not matter   mean

1 I _don't know_ the answer to this question. Can you help me?
2 What _____ you _____ of my new car? Do you like it?
3 He has a very strong accent. I _____ him.
4 I'm going to the shops. _____ you _____ anything?
5 Who _____ this coat _____ to? Is it yours?
6 'This government is terrible!'
   'I _____. They're rubbish.'
7 'I'm sorry I'm late.'
   'It _____. Don't worry.'
8 I don't know this word. What _____ it _____?
9 The United Kingdom _____ a population of over 65 million people.
10 This café is very expensive! A sandwich _____ over £8!

Adverbs of frequency

6 Put the words in the correct order.

1 cinema / I / to / often / go / friends / my / with / the
   I often go to the cinema with my friends.
2 have / toast / usually / I / breakfast / for
   _____
3 always / TV / evening / watch / I / the / in
   _____
4 holiday / often / How / do / have / you / a / ?
   _____
5 sometimes / We / Japanese / go / a / restaurant / to
   _____
6 school / I / late / never / for / am
   _____

have and have got

7 Look at the picture of **Billy**'s room and complete the conversation. Use the correct form of *have got*.

A Hi, Billy. Tell me about your bedroom. ¹_____ you _____ a lot of things in your room?
B I guess so. I ²_____ a huge TV and a laptop.
A What type of laptop ³_____ you _____?
B It's a Dell.
A And I suppose you ⁴_____ a PlayStation?
B No, I ⁵_____ one at the moment – it broke! But I prefer real games anyway. I love golf.
A ⁶_____ you _____ your own golf clubs?
B No, I use Dad's. He ⁷_____ some really nice ones.

🔊 2.3 Listen and check.

8 Rewrite the sentences using the other form of *have* or *have got*.

1 Do you have the time, please?
   Have you got the time, please?
2 I've got a terrible headache.
   _____
3 Have you got any aspirin?
   _____
4 You have a beautiful house.
   _____
5 Sally's got a really good job.
   _____
6 We haven't got any money.
   _____

Unit 2 • Let's get together   13

Present Simple and Continuous

What does she do?/ What's she doing now?

9 Look at the photos and answer the questions.

I'm Serena. I'm a football coach.

1 What does Serena do?
   <u>*She's a football coach.*</u>

2 Where does she work?
   _____ at a football club.

3 Is she working now?
   _____

4 What's she doing?
   _____ to some children.

I'm James. I'm a journalist.

5 What does James do?
   _____

6 What does he write?
   _____ articles for a newspaper.

7 Is he working now?
   _____

8 What's he doing?
   _____

10 Choose the correct form of the verb.

1 I ____ to work now. See you later.
   a 'm going   **b** go

2 We ____ the news on TV every evening.
   a 're watching   **b** watch

3 Don't turn the TV off, I ____ it!
   a watch   **b** 'm watching

4 Carla's Italian. She ____ from Milan.
   a 's coming   **b** comes

5 ____ Spanish food? I love tapas.
   a Do you like   **b** Are you liking

6 I ____ any pets.
   a 'm not having   **b** don't have

7 Don't wait for Erik. He ____.
   a doesn't come   **b** isn't coming

8 What's the matter? Why ____ crying?
   a are you   **b** do you

11 Correct the mistakes in these sentences.

1 ~~I'm liking~~ black coffee.   *I like*

2 The sun always is rising in the east.

3 I look for a white shirt in medium. Have you got any?

4 'Where's Dave?'
   'He's over there. He talks to Angela.'

5 She's 21 years old! I'm not believing her!

6 I'm learn English for my job.

7 Why you going out without a coat? It's freezing!

8 My father work in a bank.

9 I see my friends later this evening.

10 What is this word mean?

14   Unit 2 • Let's get together

Living with sheep

12 Look at the job advert.
1. What job is it for?
2. What experience do you need?

> **The opportunity of a lifetime!**
> **ASSISTANT SHEPHERD NEEDED**
> A part-time job to assist a shepherd, managing 2,000 sheep in Snowdonia National Park.
> Experience in dog training is essential.
> £11/hour   20 hours a week

13 Read about **Owen Jones**. Put the verbs in brackets in the correct form.

The Life of a Welsh Shepherd

Standing on a busy train on a rainy Monday morning, many city workers ¹ _dream_ (dream) of a life away from the crowds. Looking after sheep miles away from any other human being may sound like the perfect escape. However, the life of a shepherd isn't just about watching the sunset and walking in pretty countryside. It's often a lonely and difficult job.

Owen Jones is a Welsh shepherd. He ² _____ (spend) 12 hours a day, seven days a week, with his sheep in Snowdonia National Park. Apart from his sheep, he only has two dogs for company, Flo and Ben.

'On the good days I'm a very happy man', says Owen. 'When I ³ _____ (walk) with my dogs on a soft summer's evening, with the beauty of the mountains around me, life is perfect. But, I sometimes ⁴ _____ (not see) another human being for a whole week. My sheep and my dogs are my only friends.'

Owen ⁵ _____ (own) over 2,000 sheep and ⁶ _____ (walk) hundreds of miles. It's hard work, and so now he ⁷ _____ (look) for someone to help him. He ⁸ _____ (offer) to pay £11 an hour and he ⁹ _____ (provide) accommodation – a small cabin set in the foothills of Mount Snowdon.

The job description calls it the opportunity of a lifetime, but this job isn't just about beautiful scenery. You have to be strong, hard-working, and enjoy your own company. Sometimes you ¹⁰ _____ (not speak) to another human being for days.

'In the winter I ¹¹ _____ (work) for months on end in the rain and snow', says Owen. 'It's freezing and very lonely. Also, the newborn lambs sometimes ¹² _____ (die) of the cold – it breaks my heart, and that's when I ¹³ _____ (not like) this job.'

Many of us ¹⁴ _____ (want) to work for ourselves when we ¹⁵ _____ (have) problems with our bosses. But as Owen explains, a shepherd's boss is the weather, and it's not always a kind one. When you're on a mountain and the snow ¹⁶ _____ (fall) heavily, and you can't find your sheep, there's no one to complain to. You're on your own!

So, do you still want to escape the city and work outdoors in the countryside? Perhaps the grass isn't always greener there …

14 Complete the questions.
1. '_What do_ many city workers _dream_ of?'
   'A life away from the crowds.'
2. '_____ Owen _____ for company?'
   'Two dogs, Flo and Ben.'
3. '_____ Owen _____ for?'
   'Someone to help him.'
4. '_____ Owen _____ to pay?'
   '£11 an hour.'
5. '_____ accommodation?'
   'Yes, he is. A small cabin.'
6. '_____ Owen always _____ his job?'
   'No, he doesn't. Sometimes he's very lonely.'
7. '_____ many people _____ to quit their jobs?'
   'Because of their bosses.'
8. '_____ your boss when you're a shepherd?'
   'The weather!'

🔊 **2.4** Listen and check.

Unit 2 • Let's get together   15

Vocabulary
Things I like doing

1 Underline the correct verb.
1. I love *going* / playing to the gym.
2. I always *have* / do a lie-in on Sunday morning.
3. Karen loves *going out* / going with her friends on Saturday night.
4. I do / *take* photos on my phone all the time.

5. My parents love *watching* / seeing detective programmes on TV.
6. I love chatting / *meeting* my friends for a drink after work.

2 Complete the sentences with the correct form of the verbs in the box.

| do shop have play go read |

1. I like __going__ out with my friends at the weekend.
2. Do you like __playing__ games on your phone?
3. I __read__ the newspaper every morning. I like to know what's happening around the world.
4. I hate __doing__ nothing. I like to be busy all the time.
5. My sister loves __shopping__ for clothes. She's got two wardrobes full of new clothes.
6. At weekends, we often __have__ a barbecue in the garden.

3 EXTENSION Make a compound noun with an -ing form in **A** and a noun in **B**. Complete the sentences.

A	B
~~running~~	table
swimming	list
parking	machine
sparkling	licence
dining	water
driving	costume
shopping	~~shoes~~
washing	ticket

1. **A** I need some new __running shoes__; these have holes in them. But they're so expensive!
   B The sports shop in town has a good sale on at the moment, try there.
2. **A** How long have you had your _____ for?
   B 12 years. And I've never had an accident!
3. **A** My son's back from university with all his dirty clothes and the _____ isn't working!
   B Oh no! Just when you need it.
4. **A** I'm really thirsty. Can I have a large glass of _____, please?
   B Of course.
5. **A** My new _____ can sit ten people round it.
   B That's good. When are you having us round for dinner?
6. **A** Don't forget to pack your _____. There's an outdoor pool at the hotel.
   B I won't. I think I'll bring two.
7. **A** Leila parked on a double yellow line for just two minutes and got a _____.
   B Oh dear! She must be so cross.
8. **A** Can you put milk and bread on the _____?
   B Anything else? I think we need some orange juice, too!

🔊 **2.5** Listen and check.

Everyday English
Making conversation

Complete the conversation.

H Hi. My name's Harry. I'm a friend of Marco's.
C Hi, Harry. I'm Carolina, I'm a friend of Marco's, too. How do you ¹_____ Marco?
H We're in the same maths class at college.
C Oh really! ² _____ _____ enjoying your maths classes?
H No, they're really difficult, and I don't like all the homework.
C Marco says the same, but he likes the teacher. ³_____ you?
H Oh, yes! Professor Morris is brilliant! She's so clever. What are you ⁴_____ ?
C I'm studying Spanish and history.
H Really! ⁵_____ interesting. Can you ⁶_____ Spanish fluently?
C Well, I'm quite good, but I still make mistakes.
H I bet you're great. Have you heard of that new Spanish restaurant in town? The 'El Toro'?
C The bull! Yes, it looks good.
H How ⁷_____ going there one night? You could help me learn Spanish. *Mi español es terrible!*
C Yes, I'd ⁸_____ to.
H How about next Friday? I'll ring and book a table.
C OK. Lovely!

🔊 2.6 Listen and check.

Go online for more skills and language practice.

REVIEW
Grammar

1 Write the third person singular of these verbs.
1. live — *lives*
2. work _____
3. enjoy _____
4. play _____
5. watch _____
6. relax _____
7. study _____
8. try _____
9. go _____
10. do _____

2 Write the *-ing* form of these verbs.
1. rain — *raining*
2. go _____
3. come _____
4. swim _____
5. leave _____
6. stop _____
7. run _____
8. take _____
9. begin _____
10. travel _____

3 Correct the mistakes in these sentences.
1. Vince drive ten miles to work every day.
2. What languages does Lydia speaks?
3. I studying Japanese at Manchester University.
4. I not like fish.
5. Brad and Glen is playing football in the garden.
6. My brother always have a cup of tea in the morning.
7. Has got Ross any brothers or sisters?
8. Fiona no has any children.
9. The phone rings. Who could it be this late?
10. Karen is always having the latest designer jeans.

Go online to Check your progress.

Unit 2 • Let's get together

3 Good news, bad news!

- Past Simple
- Past Continuous
- Past Simple and Continuous
- Adverbs
- have + noun
- Saying when

Grammar
Past Simple

Positive

1 Read about **Tony Hawks**'s Irish adventure. Complete the text with the regular or irregular Past Simple form of the verbs in the boxes.

Round Ireland ... with a fridge?!

| drink   decide   agree   make   buy |
| ring   ~~choose~~ |

There are many ways to travel round Ireland – by car, coach, train, or bike. One man ¹ _chose_ to hitchhike* round Ireland, but he had a very unusual travelling companion – a fridge!

On a Saturday night in the middle of winter, Tony Hawks, a British comedian, was having dinner with some old friends. They ² _____ too much red wine, and the conversation became wilder and wilder. At the end of the night he ³ _____ a crazy bet with his friend, Kevin. He ⁴ _____ to hitchhike around Ireland in one month with a fridge! The bet was only for £100.

The next day, Kevin ⁵ _____ Tony and said he could forget the bet. However, Tony loved the silliness of the idea, and he ⁶ _____ to do it!

The next month, Tony ⁷ _____ a small fridge. He was ready for his Irish adventure!

| become   set off   love   say   win   have   go   ask   want |

The trip

Tony ⁸ _____ from Cavan in Ireland. It wasn't long before a local radio DJ ⁹ _____ interested in Tony's unusual challenge. He ¹⁰ _____ Tony to call the radio show every morning and share his travel stories with the listeners. The Irish people ¹¹ _____ hearing about his travels and wanted to help him win his bet. They called him 'the Fridge Man'.

Not surprisingly, Tony and his fridge ¹² _____ some interesting adventures. They had tea with the king of Tory Island, a tiny Irish-speaking island off the coast of Donegal. Tony ¹³ _____ to win the princess's hand in marriage with a bunch of flowers, but unfortunately the princess was away. He also ¹⁴ _____ surfing with Bingo, one of Ireland's champion surfers. Bingo ¹⁵ _____ the fridge was a better surfer than Tony!

Tony loved the warmth and generosity of the Irish people. He found it amazing that a small fridge could bring so many people together. And he ¹⁶ _____ the bet!

The king of Tory Island

hitchhike to travel by getting free lifts from passing cars

Questions

2 Write the questions about Tony Hawks.
1. 'What _did Tony travel round Ireland_ with?' 'A fridge.'
2. 'Who _____ with?' 'His friend, Kevin.'
3. 'How long _____ the journey _____?' 'It took one month.'
4. 'How much _____ for?' '£100.'
5. 'Why _____ he decide _____?' 'Because he loved the silliness of the idea.'
6. 'Where _____ from?' 'Cavan.'
7. 'What _____?' 'The Fridge Man.'
8. 'Who _____ with?' 'The king of Tory Island.'

🔊 **3.1** Listen and check.

Negatives and short answers

3 Correct the information.
1. Tony met his friends on a Friday night.
   Tony didn't meet his friends on a Friday night.
   He met them on a Saturday night.
2. Tony drank too much beer.
   _____
3. He had six weeks to complete the bet.
   _____
4. The bet was for £1,000.
   _____
5. During his trip, Tony went skydiving.
   _____

4 Answer the questions with short answers.
1. 'Did he travel with a washing machine?'
   ' _No, he didn't._ '
2. 'Did he travel round Scotland?'
   ' _____ '
3. 'Did he meet lots of friendly people on his trip?'
   ' _____ '
4. 'Did he get married?' ' _____ '
5. 'Did he go surfing?' ' _____ '
6. 'Did he lose the bet?' ' _____ '

🔊 **3.2** Listen and check.

Past Continuous

5 This is what you saw when you arrived at work yesterday. Write sentences in the Past Continuous.

When I arrived at work ...
1. Claude and Ellie / chat / next to / photocopier
   Claude and Ellie were chatting next to the photocopier.
2. Penny / eat / cake
   Penny was eating the cake.
3. Martin / drink / coffee
   Martin was drinking coffee.
4. Molly / shop / online
   Molly was shoping online.
5. Andy and Matt / talk / last night's match
   Andy and Matt were talking last night's match.

6 Complete the questions about the people in the picture.
1. 'Who _was_ Claude _talking_ to?' 'Ellie.'
2. 'What _was_ Penny _eating_?' 'A cake.'
3. 'What _were_ you _wearing_, Molly?' 'A new dress.'
4. 'What _were_ you _talking_ to Matt about, Andy?' 'The match.'

7 Complete the negative sentences.
1. Martin _wasn't drinking_ (not drink) tea.
2. Claude and Ellie _weren't using_ (not use) the photocopier.
3. Molly _wasn't doing_ (not do) any work.
4. Andy and Matt _weren't talking_ (not talk) about work.

Unit 3 • Good news, bad news! 19

News stories

8 Read the three stories. Put the phrases in the box in the correct place in the stories.

> a and was waiting for him at the finish line
> b who were all watching its final journey
> c because he was going to visit his mother
> d while travelling at 141,600 kilometres per hour
> e who was driving dangerously
> f while he was running

Blind Driver Arrested

Police in Kentucky stopped a 31-year-old man, Daniel McCarthy, ¹____, and then discovered he was blind. 'He had his dog with him,' said police spokesman Melvyn Kittburg. McCarthy said he only recently lost his sight. He knew the road very well ²____. His dog was trained to bark once at a red light and twice at a green light. McCarthy lost his driving licence.

The 100-Year-Old Marathon Runner

Fauja Singh became the first 100-year-old to finish a marathon when he completed the Toronto Waterfront marathon in 8 hours 11 minutes and 5.9 seconds. He drank lots of water ³____ and he never took a rest. Fauja was exhausted after the race, and said the last six miles were the most difficult. His 75-year-old son came to the race ⁴____.

Fauja started running at the age of 89 after the deaths of his wife, son and daughter. It gave him a reason to live.

Death of a Spacecraft: Cassini Hits Saturn

NASA's Cassini spacecraft ended its 20-year mission when it dived into Saturn. Cassini, a man-made meteor, hit Saturn at 11.30 a.m. UK time ⁵____. This moment marked the end of an eight-billion-kilometre journey. NASA scientists and engineers, ⁶____, were very emotional. Many of them were at NASA 20 years ago when Cassini started its journey.

Past Simple and Continuous

9 Write the verbs once in the Past Simple and once in the Past Continuous.

have

1 'I went to Liam's party last night.'
   '_Did_ you _have_ a good time?'
2 They _were having_ dinner when the doorbell rang.

live

3 I _____ in Rome when I was a child.
4 I _____ in Rome when I met my wife.

talk

5 You were on the phone for ages! Who _____ you _____ to?
6 I had a problem with my neighbour, but I _____ to him, and it's OK now.

wear

7 When I saw Bella, she _____ a beautiful red dress – she looked stunning.
8 'What _____ you _____ for your interview yesterday?'
   'A suit and tie.'

rain

9 When I left the house, it _____, so I took my umbrella.
10 'Did you have good weather for your wedding?'
   'No, it _____ all day, but it didn't matter.'

The 'White Mouse'

10 Read the introduction to the text about **Nancy Wake**.
1 Who was she?   2 What nickname did the Gestapo give her?

11 Read the full text. <u>Underline</u> the correct form of the verb.

Nancy Wake – soldier and spy

Nancy Wake was a World War II soldier and spy. During the war the Gestapo gave her the nickname the 'White Mouse' because she was so difficult to catch.

Nancy was born in New Zealand, but she ¹*was growing up / grew up* in Australia. At the age of 20, she left Australia and travelled to London, New York, and Paris. She settled down in France and married a Frenchman, Henri Fiocca. They ²*were living / lived* in Marseille when the war started. Nancy joined the French Resistance and helped a lot of people escape the country. The Gestapo ³*was finding / found* out about Nancy and she ⁴*was becoming / became* their most wanted person. They looked for the 'White Mouse' everywhere, but she managed to escape from France to the UK. Her husband ⁵*was preparing / prepared* to join her in London, but unfortunately, the Gestapo ⁶*were finding / found* him and shot him.

When Nancy got to England, she joined the Special Operations Executive (SOE) and became a fully trained agent in only eight months. After her training, she went to France on a mission. Soon, Nancy ⁷*was fighting / fought* with the men in some of the fiercest battles. 'I liked that kind of thing', she said.

Nancy was a cool character. One day, while she ⁸*was eating / ate* her breakfast, she ⁹*was ordering / ordered* a soldier to shoot an enemy spy. 'It didn't put me off* my breakfast,' she said!

After the liberation of France, Nancy ¹⁰*was returning / returned* to London. She received nine medals from the British, French and American governments, including the George Medal, the Croix de Guerre, and the Médaille de la Résistance.

She died on August 7, 2011, three weeks before her 99th birthday.

put somebody off make somebody dislike something

12 Complete the questions and write the answers.

1 Where / Nancy / born?
<u>Where was Nancy born?</u>
<u>In New Zealand.</u>

2 When / leave / Australia?
_____
_____

3 Where / live / when the war started?
_____
_____

4 Why / the Gestapo / want to find her?
_____
_____

5 Where / go / after the liberation of France?
_____
_____

6 How many / medals / receive?
_____
_____

🔊 **3.3** Listen and check.

Unit 3 • Good news, bad news!   21

Vocabulary
Adverbs

1 Find the verb and adverb pairs.

verb	adverb
~~drive~~	regularly
work	passionately
wait	clearly
exercise	~~slowly~~
explain	brightly
fight	patiently
shine	hard
love	bravely

1 _drive slowly_
2 _____
3 _____
4 _____
5 _____
6 _____
7 _____
8 _____

2 Complete the sentences with a verb and adverb combination from **1** in the correct form.
1 The sun _was shining brightly_ when we left home this morning, but by lunchtime it was raining.
2 My dog, Pedro, _____ for me outside the supermarket while I went shopping.
3 It's very icy, please _____. The roads are really dangerous.
4 Romeo and Juliet _____ each other so _____.
5 I have a really good maths teacher. She always _____ things so _____.
6 Nicola _____ really _____ for her exams, and passed them all.
7 The American Indians _____ against the cowboys.
8 I want to be healthy and fit so I _____ _____.

have + noun

have is often used with a noun to express an action.
 I was **having a bath** when the phone rang.
 We **had lunch** in an Italian restaurant.
Notice that we don't use *a* with meals.
 I **had breakfast** and went to work.

3 **EXTENSION** Complete the sentences with a form of *have* and a noun from the box.

| ~~an argument~~   a look   a dream   a swim   a word |
| a shower   a break   a good time   a drink |

1 I couldn't sleep last night. My neighbours _had an argument_, and I could hear every word.
2 I was tired when I got home, so I _____, washed my hair and went to bed.
3 'I went to a party last night.'
 'Oh! Was it good? Did you _____?'
4 I _____ about you last night. I dreamt you were the Prime Minister.
5 Can I _____ at your wedding photos?
6 It's so hot! I think I'll _____ in the pool before lunch.
7 Are you thirsty? Would you like to _____?
8 Can I _____ with you? There's something I need to talk to you about.
9 I need a coffee. Can we _____ soon?

Everyday English
Saying when

1 Complete the conversations with *in*, *at*, *on* or – (no preposition).

1. **A** What time does the film start?
   B <u>At</u> six o'clock.
2. **A** When were you born?
   B I was born _____ 1998.
3. **A** Hooray! It's Friday! Nearly the weekend!
   B I can't wait to finish work. I'm going out _____ this evening.
4. **A** My driving test is _____ Thursday.
   B Good luck!
5. **A** What did you do _____ the weekend?
   B I went to a birthday party _____ Saturday night. It was amazing!
6. **A** We always go on holiday _____ July.
   B We usually go away _____ winter. We visit my family in Australia.
7. **A** You look tired. Did you go to bed late _____ last night?
   B Yeah. I went out with friends and didn't get home until two o'clock _____ the morning.

🔊 **3.4** Listen and check.

2 Complete the conversation with words from the box.

| in   at (x2)   on (x2)   last   ago   when |

A When's your birthday?
B It's ¹ <u>on</u> 13 September.
A What year were you born?
B I was born ² _____ 1996. When's *your* birthday?
A It was a couple of weeks ³ _____ , actually.
B Really? What did you do ⁴ _____ your birthday?
A Not much. ⁵ _____ I was 21, I had a huge party with fireworks ⁶ _____ midnight, and ⁷ _____ year we went to a club, but this year was very quiet.
B We're having a party for Sally's birthday. It's next Saturday ⁸ _____ 8.00. Do you want to come?
A Great! I'd love to!

🔊 **3.5** Listen and check.

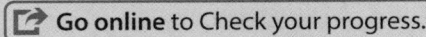

REVIEW
Grammar

1 Complete the table.

		Past Simple	Past Continuous
1	study	*studied*	*was/were studying*
2	live		
3	ring		
4	leave		
5	plan		
6	try		
7	travel		
8	make		

2 <u>Underline</u> the correct form of the verb in the text.

One day, Margot Clements ¹*was walking / walked* along the High Street. It was hot so she decided to take off her coat. While she ²*was taking it off / took it off*, her phone ³*was starting / started* to ring. She ⁴*was opening / opened* her bag to answer it. The phone ⁵*was ringing / rang* loudly, but she couldn't find it anywhere. She ⁶*was putting / put* her bag down on a bench.

Suddenly, a man ⁷*was appearing / appeared* from nowhere. He ⁸*was picking up / picked up* her bag and ⁹*was running / ran* down the road with it. A policeman ¹⁰*was stopping / stopped* him because the phone ¹¹*was still ringing / still rang*, and he wanted to know why the man didn't answer it!

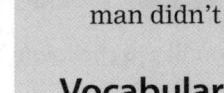

Vocabulary

3 Rewrite the sentence using the opposite adverb.

1. I went to bed late.   I <u>didn't go to bed early</u>.
2. My sister can't type very fast.
   She _____.
3. Don't speak so loudly.
   Can you _____?
4. Chris drives dangerously.
   He doesn't _____.
5. I don't sleep heavily.
   I sleep _____.

Unit 3 • Good news, bad news! 23

4 Food for thought

- Countable and uncountable nouns
- Expressions of quantity
- Pronouns – *something/no one* …
- Articles – *a/an*, *the* or –?
- A piece of cake; Shops
- Can you come for dinner?

Grammar
Countable and uncountable nouns

1 Write the nouns in the correct column.

| ~~apple~~ ~~sugar~~ stamp car petrol meat water money dollar change rice job work potato fruit soup bread news information |

Countable nouns	Uncountable nouns
apple	sugar

2 **EXTENSION** Sometimes a noun can be countable and uncountable. Look at the photos and complete the sentences with *a* + noun or just the noun.

1 I like _chocolate_.   2 Would you like _a chocolate_?

3 I love _____.   4 Can I have _____?

5 It's made of _____.   6 It's _____ of wine.

3 **EXTENSION** Complete the sentences with *some* + noun or *a/an* + noun.

Can you buy me _a paper_?   I need _some paper_.

I'd like _____, please.   Would you like _____?

Have _____!   Can I have _____?

Expressions of quantity

some or any?

4 Complete the sentences with *some* or *any*.

1. There isn't _____ milk in the fridge.
2. Is there _____ petrol in the car?
3. Can you buy _____ milk when you go out?
4. I didn't buy _____ grapes.
5. I need to get _____ petrol on my way to work.
6. I need _____ change for the parking meter.
7. I haven't got _____ money.
8. Can you lend me _____ money?
9. Can you give me _____ advice?
10. Did you have _____ problems with this exercise?

How much or How many?

5 Complete the questions with *How much* or *How many*.

1. '_____ children do you have?'
   'Three. Two boys and a girl.'
2. '_____ butter do we need?'
   'Just one pack.'
3. '_____ eggs did you buy?'
   'Half a dozen.'
4. '_____ people are coming to the party?'
   'About forty.'
5. '_____ do you earn?'
   'That's none of your business!'
6. '_____ bedrooms are there in your house?'
   'Three.'

🔊 **4.1** Listen and check.

much, many or a lot of?

6 Look at the picture. Complete the sentences with *much* or *many*. When *much* or *many* are not possible, use *a lot of*.

	Positive	Negative	Questions
Countable	a lot of	many / a lot of	many / a lot of
Uncountable	a lot of	much / a lot of	much / a lot of

1. The shop has **a lot of** apples.
2. I can't see **much** bread.
3. There aren't _____ sweets.
4. Have they got _____ cheese?
5. There's _____ sugar.
6. There aren't _____ spices.
7. There isn't _____ milk.
8. There are _____ yoghurts.
9. They don't have _____ butter.
10. There are _____ cans of Cola.
11. There isn't _____ olive oil.
12. There's _____ rice.

a few or a little?

7 Match a question in **A** with a reply in **B** and **C**.

A	B	C
1 'Does your tooth hurt?'		'I'm trying to lose weight.'
2 'Were there many people at the party?'	'Just a few.' 'Just a little.'	'But I'm going to the dentist tomorrow.'
3 'Have some cream with your dessert!'		'The children ate most of them yesterday.'
4 'Have you got any chocolate biscuits?'		'I didn't know anyone.'

🔊 **4.2** Listen and check.

Pronouns – something/no one …

8 Complete each pair of sentences with the correct word.

someone   anyone

1 There's _someone_ on the phone for you.
2 Did _anyone_ ring me last night?

everything   nothing

3 She has _____ – a rich husband and a big house.
4 He has _____ – not a penny to his name.

somewhere   everywhere

5 I can't find my keys! I've looked _____.
6 I want to go on holiday – _____ hot.

anyone   no one

7 'Who did you speak to at the party?'
'_____. I just stayed for ten minutes, then I left.'
8 I couldn't see _____ I knew at the party, so I left.

someone   everyone

9 It was a great concert! _____ enjoyed it.
10 Could _____ lend me £20 till the end of the week?

9 Complete the sentences with a combination of words from the table.

some any no every	+	one thing where

1 Does _anyone_ know whose book this is?
2 Please don't worry about me. I'm fine. _____'s the matter.
3 Is there _____ I can do to help?
4 I'm so unhappy. _____ loves me.
5 I put my glasses _____ safe, and now I can't find them.
6 We're going to sing 'Happy Birthday'. _____ has to join in.

Articles – a/an, the, or –?

10 Complete the sentences with a/an or the.

1 Pat and Aron are **a** lovely couple. She has **a** shop and he's **an** engineer.
2 We went to _____ cinema to see _____ film about Martin Luther King.
3 It was my friend's birthday yesterday. I bought her _____ bunch of flowers and _____ box of chocolates. She put _____ flowers in _____ lovely vase.
4 'Where are _____ children?'
'They're playing in _____ garden.'
5 'Where are my shoes?'
'They're on _____ floor in _____ kitchen.'
6 I'd love to live in _____ house with _____ balcony near _____ sea.
7 Before you go to bed, can you feed _____ cat and turn off _____ lights?
8 We drove to _____ Lake District last weekend and found _____ lovely restaurant next to Lake Windermere. _____ food was excellent.

11 Match a noun in **A** with a verb in **B** and an ending in **C** to make general statements.

A	B	C
1 Bees	eat	lies.
2 Children	play	honey.
3 Mechanics	make	cars.
4 Politicians	mend	with toys.
5 Butchers	tell	fish.
6 Cats	sell	meat.

12 Correct the mistakes in the sentences.

1 Last night we had ~~the~~ dinner in ₐ restaurant.
2 I come to the school by the bus.
3 I had the lunch with Michael yesterday.
4 My sister's doctor.
5 We have best teacher in world.
6 I usually go to the bed at midnight.

Unit 4 • Food for thought

Fish and chips

13 Read the text and complete the sentences.
1. _The Belgians_ invented chips.
2. _____ was the first person to sell fish and chips in London.
3. _____ wrote about fish and chips.
4. _____ opened the biggest fish and chip shop in the world in 1931.
5. _____ serves fish and chips in his restaurant in Paris.

Britain's favourite meal

The Portuguese gave us fried fish. The Belgians invented chips. Then more than 150 years ago, the British put them together to create fish and chips.

Today, Britain has lots of fish and chip shops – over 10,500! They make over £1.2 billion a year. However, this multi-million-pound industry grew from small beginnings.

How it all began

150 years ago, on the streets of the East End of London, a 13-year-old boy called Joseph Malin had the bright idea of combining fried fish with chips.

Joseph's family didn't have much money, so to increase the family income they began frying chips in a downstairs room of their house. Nearby was a fried fish shop, and Joseph put some fried fish with his chips and walked the streets. He sold the fish and chips from a tray, which hung round his neck. Joseph sold lots of fish and chips, so he decided to open a fish and chip shop – the first of many fish and chip shops in Britain.

Fish and chips became a favourite with poor people. They didn't cost much money and they were quick and tasty. Charles Dickens, the famous Victorian novelist, wrote about 'fried fish warehouses' in his book *Oliver Twist*.

The dispute

However, there are some questions about how the dish really began. In the north of England a lot of people don't believe Joseph Malin's story. They say a man called John Lees began selling fish and chips in a market in Mossley, Lancashire in 1863. Today, there is a plaque there in his honour.

Whatever the truth, the dish became extremely popular. By 1910 there were more than 25,000 shops across the country and over 35,000 by the 1920s. In 1931 Harry Ramsden from Yorkshire opened a fish and chip shop 'palace' modelled on the Ritz Hotel in London. Lots of people visited the original shop. There are now Harry Ramsden's fish and chip shops all over the world.

Fish and chips today

Nowadays, there are many other kinds of fast food, such as burgers, kebabs, and pizzas. They are much more popular than fish and chips. However, in Paris, France, *le fish and chips* is becoming the chic new meal. It appears on menus in some of Paris's most fashionable restaurants. 'People love them for lunch or supper,' says chef Olivier Dupart.

14 Are the sentences true (✓) or false (✗)? Correct the false ones using *much*, *many* or *a lot of*.

1. ✗ There aren't many fish and chip shops in Britain.
   There are a lot of fish and chip shops in Britain.
2. ✓ They make a lot of money.
3. ☐ Joseph's family was poor.
4. ☐ Joseph sold a lot of fish and chips.
5. ☐ Fish and chips were expensive.
6. ☐ Some people in the north of England don't believe Joseph Malin's story.
7. ☐ Today, pizza and burgers are much more popular than fish and chips.

15 Join the lines about *Britain's favourite meal* with *a*, *an*, *the* or no article (–).

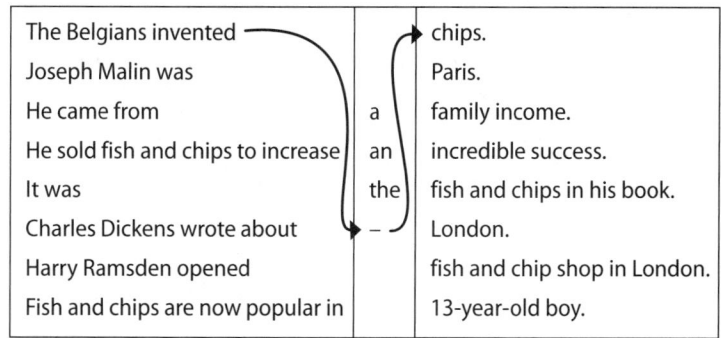

Unit 4 • Food for thought   27

Vocabulary
A piece of cake

1 Write a word from the box before the nouns. There may be more than one possible answer.

| slice   packet   can   bunch   loaf   bottle   piece   box |

1 a *piece/slice* of cake
2 a _____ of ham
3 a _____ of beer
4 a _____ of bananas
5 a _____ of crisps
6 a _____ of olive oil
7 a _____ of paper
8 a _____ of Coke
9 a _____ of grapes
10 a _____ of chocolates
11 a _____ of chewing gum
12 a _____ of flowers
13 a _____ of bread
14 a _____ of biscuits
15 a _____ of tissues

Shops

2 Look at the picture of a street in a town. Where can you get the things on the list?

1 a loaf of bread   *baker's*
2 a book of stamps   _____
3 some meat   _____
4 a newspaper   _____
5 a packet of aspirin _____
6 an English dictionary _____
7 some money   _____
8 a bottle of wine   _____

Food

3 **EXTENSION** Write the words in the correct column. There are five words for each column.

| ~~chicken~~   lemon   melon   ham   peach   courgette   beef   pea   carrot
turkey   onion   raspberry   lamb   pineapple   cauliflower |

Vegetables	Fruit	Meat
		chicken

28 Unit 4 • Food for thought

Everyday English
Can you come for dinner?

1 Complete the conversations.

1. **A** Would you _____ passing the potatoes, please?
   B No, not _____ _____. Shall I serve you some?
   A That's plenty. Thank you.

2. **A** _____ for seconds?
   B No, thanks. I couldn't eat _____ thing!

3. **A** Has anyone got _____ for more strawberry cheesecake?
   B Yes, please. Seconds _____ me.
   A Here you are. You've got the last slice.

4. **A** _____ you pour me a glass of water, please?
   B Still or _____?
   A Still, please.

5. **A** _____ would you like your coffee?
   B With milk, but no sugar, please. And have you got _____ decaf?
   A No, sorry.

🔊 **4.3** Listen and check.

2 Put the words in order to make requests.

1. £20 / me / you / lend / Can / ?
   _____
2. your / I / take / Can / coat / ?
   _____
3. me / password / Could / tell / the / Wi-fi / you / ?
   _____
4. tea / I / another / of / Can / cup / have / ?
   _____
5. have / house / I / the / a / Can / of / wine / glass / ?
   _____
6. home / lift / you / me / Can / give / a / ?
   _____

▶ **Go online** for more skills and language practice.

REVIEW
Grammar

1 <u>Underline</u> the correct words in the conversation.
   A Good morning! Can I help you?
   B Yes. I'd like ¹*some / any* grapes, please. How ²*much / many* are they?
   A £4 a kilo.
   B OK. I'd like ³*a / –* big bunch, please. And do you have ⁴*some / any* bananas?
   A I've only got ⁵*a little / a few* left – just three.
   B OK. Never mind. I need some vegetables, too. Can I have ⁶*some / any* broccoli?
   A It's just over there – help yourself. ⁷*Something / Anything* else?
   B Er, some spinach, perhaps. Just ⁸*a few / a little*. How ⁹*much / many* is that altogether?
   A That's £7.50, please.

🔊 **4.4** Listen and check.

2 Correct the mistakes in these sentences.
1. There are too much children in my daughter's class.
2. Adam has a new job. He's making so many money!
3. I don't eat the fish because I don't like it.
4. There isn't some chicken in my chicken pie!
5. It's Fred's party tonight and I don't have something to wear!
6. I had a lazy day yesterday. I didn't do nothing!
7. Could I have any milk in my tea, please?
8. I came to work by car this morning. Fortunately, there wasn't many traffic.
9. What did you have for the breakfast?
10. Could I have the lift to school, please?

3 Write the plural forms of these nouns.

1. carrot _____   6. family _____
2. potato _____   7. child _____
3. peach _____   8. boy _____
4. fruit _____   9. person _____
5. lemon _____   10. man _____

▶ **Go online** to Check your progress.

Unit 4 • Food for thought   29

Stop and check Units 1–4

Grammar

1 Choose the correct answer.

1 _____ are you doing?
   a Where
   b Who
   c What

2 Odette is French. She _____ from Marseille.
   a come
   b comes
   c is coming

3 _____ Jess and Craig going out together?
   a Do
   b Are
   c Is

4 Does she _____ dark or fair hair?
   a got
   b have
   c has

5 I _____ Italian at evening classes at the moment.
   a learn
   b learning
   c 'm learning

6 Where exactly is Lena living _____ London?
   a by
   b at
   c in

7 I _____ all my homework before I went to bed.
   a did
   b do
   c was doing

8 _____ do you get to school?
   a What
   b Where
   c How

9 He's living back home with his parents _____.
   a nowadays
   b often
   c at the moment

10 _____ dog is that? Yours?
   a Whose
   b Who's
   c Which

11 What _____ make for dinner tonight?
   a do you
   b are you going
   c are you going to

12 My sister _____ got long dark hair.
   a doesn't
   b hasn't
   c haven't

13 I saw Tina at the party, she _____ a lovely red dress.
   a wore
   b weared
   c was wearing

14 You _____ a word I said!
   a don't hear
   b didn't hear
   c didn't listen

15 I don't know _____ your keys are.
   a how many
   b where
   c whose

16 I lost my wallet while I _____.
   a shopped
   b was shopping
   c went shopping

17 We _____ the party before it ended.
   a left
   b were leaving
   c leaved

18 I don't want _____ broccoli. I don't like it.
   a some
   b any
   c many

19 We've only got _____ eggs left.
   a a little
   b a few
   c few

20 She checks her phone about ten times _____ hour!
   a the
   b an
   c a

SCORE   20

30 Stop and check • Units 1–4

Vocabulary

2 Use the clues to complete the crossword.

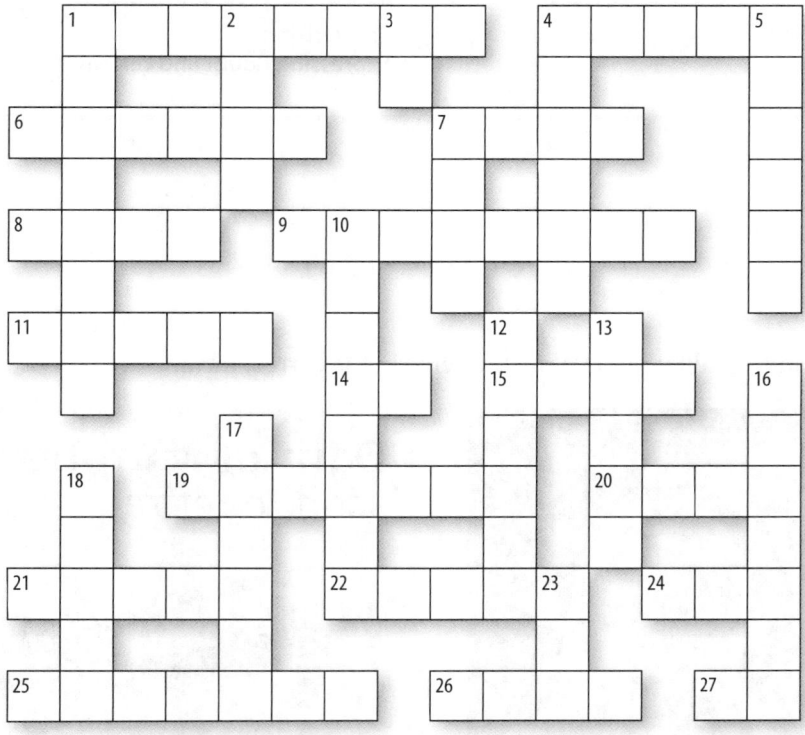

ACROSS

1 A place where you can buy books. (8)
4 Dan gave me a lovely big _____ of flowers. (5)
6 His English is good, but he has a _____ accent. (6)
7 You can't _____ your car here. (4)
8 I try not to _____ online – I buy too many things! (4)
9 Excuse me, what's the Wi-fi _____ for this café? (8)
11 Mmm! That loaf of _____ looks delicious! (5)
14 I was born in Germany, but I grew _____ in Italy. (2)
15 _____ luck in your exam tomorrow! (4)
19 To rent a car, you need to show your driving _____. (7)
20 Get a piece of cake quickly – there isn't much _____! (4)
21 That's enough work – let's have a coffee _____! (5)
22 *Met* is the past _____ of *meet*. (5)
24 The weather was terrible on Saturday – it rained _____ day! (3)
25 I _____ work at 8.00 a.m. and didn't finish till 9.00 p.m.! (7)
26 Can you help me _____ this crossword, please. It's not easy! (4)
27 Anna and Don are working in Africa _____ volunteers. (2)

DOWN

1 I need to buy some meat from the _____. (8)
2 What _____ of food do you like? (4)
3 Can I have a bunch _____ grapes, please? (2)
4 Can I _____ your bike for an hour? I need to go into town quickly. (6)
5 I wouldn't like to play ice _____ – it looks easy to get injured! (6)
7 Could you take these letters to the _____ office? (4)
10 Jim and I aren't speaking – we had a big _____ yesterday. (8)
12 Joe said I was wrong at first, but he _____ with me now. (6)
13 In the US, it's a popsicle. In the UK it's an ice _____. (5)
16 I've got six _____ of wine for the party – is that enough? (7)
17 You'll get a parking _____ if you park on a double yellow line. (6)
18 That was a bad meal – the _____ I've ever eaten! (6)
23 I'm full – I couldn't _____ another thing! (3)

SCORE 30

TOTAL 50

Stop and check • Units 1–4

5 The future's in your hands

- Verb patterns
- Future forms
- Phrasal verbs
- The verb *get*
- Expressing doubt and certainty

Grammar
Verb patterns

1 Read the interviews with Maddie and Dermot. Write the verbs in the correct form.

Maddie Johnson, *climatologist to be*

I Maddie, what would you like [1] *to be* (be) when you grow up?

M I'd like [2] _____ (work) in climatology.

I Really? What does that involve?

M You study the climate. You know, the clouds, tornadoes, hurricanes, things like that.

I Wow! Why are you thinking of [3] _____ (do) that?

M Well, I'm interested in [4] _____ (learn) about global warming and how it's changing the weather, and I want [5] _____ (save) the world.

I Well, I'm very pleased [6] _____ (hear) that. I think doing climatology is a great idea. We all need [7] _____ (know) more about global warming. Good luck, Maddie!

Dermot Murphy, *soon to retire*

I Hi Dermot. What are you going to do when you retire?

D Well, I really enjoy [8] _____ (fly) planes. I've always wanted [9] _____ (be) a pilot, so I've started [10] _____ (take) flying lessons. I'm hoping [11] _____ (have) my own plane one day.

I When do you think you'll get your own plane?

D I'm trying to save enough money, but they're very expensive, so it's going [12] _____ (take) a long time.

I Which countries would you like [13] _____ (visit) first?

D Well, I'm thinking of flying to northern Spain. I want [14] _____ (see) my brother, Neil. He lives in Santander.

I Well, that sounds like a wonderful idea. Good luck, Dermot!

🔊 5.1 Listen and check.

Infinitive or -ing?

2 Complete the sentences with the infinitive or the -ing form. Sometimes both are possible.
1. I need **to get** (get) a job.
2. I hope _____ (earn) a lot of money.
3. I started _____ (learn) English two years ago.
4. We decided _____ (buy) a new car.
5. I stopped _____ (learn) the piano when I was ten.
6. She enjoys _____ (visit) new countries.
7. I'm thinking of _____ (go) travelling.
8. I'm fed up with _____ (do) the same thing every day.
9. I'm looking forward to _____ (finish) work.
10. We're trying _____ (save) money for a new house.

3 Write a sentence about each of these people's hopes and ambitions.

1. Emma / hope / be / vet / because / love / work / with animals
   Emma hopes to be a vet because she loves working with animals.
2. Sheila / want / be / teacher / because / enjoy / work / with children
   _____
3. Mike / would like / be / farmer / because / like / work / outside
   _____
4. Jim / plan / work in IT / because / want / earn / a lot of money
   _____
5. Terry / want / be / accountant / because / good at / work / with numbers
   _____
6. We / think of / buy / a cottage by the sea / because / love / sail
   _____

like or would like

4 <u>Underline</u> the correct question.
1. **A** *Would you like a drink?*
   Do you like a drink?
   B Yes, please! I'm really thirsty!
2. **A** *Do you like your teacher?*
   Would you like your teacher?
   B Yes, she's really nice.
3. **A** *Do you like going to the cinema?*
   Would you like to go to the cinema?
   B Yes, I go every week.
4. **A** *Would you like to go for a swim?*
   Do you like going swimming?
   B Yes, that's a good idea. It's so hot today.
5. **A** *Would you like to go out tonight?*
   Do you like going out in the evening?
   B Yes, let's go out for a nice meal.

🔊 **5.2** Listen and check.

5 Complete the sentences using *would like* or *like* and the verb in brackets.
1. 'What sort of books **do** you **like reading** (read)?'
   'Biographies and thrillers.'
2. 'Ryan told me you've got a new car.'
   'Yes, it's in the garage. _____ you _____ (see) it?'
3. 'Why do you have so many cook books?'
   'Because I _____ (cook)!'
4. '_____ you _____ (watch) horror films?'
   'Yes, I love the really scary ones!'
5. 'I'm so cold!'
   '_____ you _____ (borrow) a jumper?'

🔊 **5.3** Listen and check.

Unit 5 · The future's in your hands

Future forms

will and won't

6 Complete the sentences with the phrases in the box.

> 'll see   'll be   won't take   won't be
> won't recognize   'll soon feel

1 I'm going to have my hair cut short. You _____ me next time you see me.
2 On my next birthday I _____ 30. That's so old!
3 Could you help me move the furniture? It _____ long.
4 Take two of these pills a day and you _____ better.
5 'The film starts at 7.30. I'll see you outside at 7.15.'
   'Don't worry! I _____ late!'
6 Bye! Have a nice evening! I _____ you tomorrow!

will for offers and decisions

7 Complete the dialogues with *will* and a verb from the box.

> get   pay   ask   help

1 **A** That was a great meal! How much is the bill?
   B It's my turn. I _____ for this.
2 **A** This maths homework is so difficult!
   B I _____ you with it if you want.
3 **A** Tom needs to be there when we discuss the new plan.
   B OK, I _____ him to come to the meeting.
4 **A** We haven't got any food in the house!
   B It's OK – I _____ a takeaway.

🔊 **5.4** Listen and check.

What's going to happen?

8 Look at the pictures. What's going to happen? Make sentences with *going to*.

_____   _____
_____   _____

_____   _____
_____   _____

will, going to or the Present Continuous?

9 Complete the conversations. Choose the correct answer.

1 'Mum! Can you help me with my homework?'
   'Don't ask me! Ask your dad! ____ you.'
   a He'll help   **b** He's going to help
2 'Why are you cleaning the flat?'
   'Because my parents ____ tomorrow.'
   a will visit   **b** are visiting
3 'Where ____ on holiday next year?'
   'Portugal. I can't wait!'
   a will you go   **b** are you going
4 'What ____ for Karen's birthday on Saturday?'
   'I'm taking her out for dinner.'
   a are you doing   **b** will you do
5 'Oh no! Look at the time! I'm going to miss my train.'
   'Don't worry. ____ you a lift to the station.'
   a I'm giving   **b** I'll give
6 'Why are you wearing shorts and trainers?'
   'Because ____ play tennis later!'
   a I'm going to   **b** I'll go

🔊 **5.5** Listen and check.

34 Unit 5 • The future's in your hands

Mohammad Razai's story

10 Read the article quickly and answer the questions.
1 Why did Mohammad leave Afghanistan?
2 Is his life in England happy and successful?
3 What are his hopes for the future?

The refugee from Afghanistan

Twenty years ago, a boy called Mohammad Razai arrived in England with nothing but a few clothes. Today he is a graduate of Cambridge University and a medical doctor.

Aged just 15, Mohammad set out from his home country of Afghanistan with his cousin. His mother told him to leave Afghanistan when life became very dangerous for the family. 'I was very sad,' he said, 'I didn't know if I would see my mother again.' An uncle managed to get them on a plane, but they had no idea where they were going. Finally, they got to England.

When they arrived, Mohammad was very surprised at how kind people were. 'We lived with a foster family. The mother made us feel very welcome. I didn't understand how another human being could help a complete stranger.'

At his new school in England, a teacher lent him a computer and persuaded him to take an IT exam. 'All the other teachers thought it was too soon, but I passed.'

How did he learn so fast? 'I knew I had to succeed, and to succeed I had to work hard.' He passed more exams and went to University College London, where he studied biology. But his dream was to study medicine at Cambridge.

Mohammad's dream came true in 2014 when he graduated in medicine from Cambridge. He loved studying medicine so much that he decided to do a master's degree as well! He is now a British citizen and a fully qualified medical doctor.

'I love this country,' he says. 'I feel part of British society. I will get married and stay here now. I really want to do something useful. I want to show people that asylum seekers are human beings with feelings, ambitions, and dreams, just like everyone else. People don't leave their own country without a good reason. Leaving home, family, and friends and going to the other side of the world is not easy.'

Mohammad also wants to help those young people who can't start new lives in another country. He's an ambassador for One Young World and the Universal Peace Federation. He's worried about the increase in deaths from smoking in Afghanistan, and is going to do everything he can to educate young people there about the dangers of smoking.

'If people have the chance to improve their lives, they will do it with all their heart and soul', he says. 'They just need the opportunity.'

11 Read the article again and complete the sentences with the correct form of the verbs in the box.

travel find leave make educate live study take

1 Mohammad's mother told him _____. Afghanistan because it was dangerous.
2 She wanted him _____ to a safe country.
3 Mohammad was surprised _____ such kind people in England.
4 Mohammad's maths teacher persuaded him _____ an IT exam.
5 Mohammad enjoyed _____ for his degree in medicine at Cambridge University.
6 Mohammad loves _____ in Britain.
7 He wants _____ the young people of Afghanistan about the dangers of smoking.
8 He wants _____ the world a better place to live in.

12 These lines are said by people in Mohammad's story. Choose the correct form. Who do you think is saying each line?

1 '*I'm going / I going* to get you out of this country and make sure you're safe.'
2 'I'm worried *I won't ever see / I'm not ever seeing* you again.'
3 '*You're both getting / You'll both get* on a flight tomorrow.'
4 'Welcome, Mohammad. This *is going to be / is being* your new home.'
5 'Perhaps *I'll get / I'm going to get* married in the next few years.'
6 'I think *you're doing / you're going to do* well in this school in the future. *I'll lend / I'm lending* you a computer so you can take the IT exam.'
7 'I think *I'm doing / I'll do* a master's degree in medicine next.'
8 '*I'll travel / I'm travelling* to Kabul at 2.00, for an anti-smoking conference.'

Unit 5 • The future's in your hands 35

Vocabulary
Phrasal verbs

1 Complete the sentences with the verbs from the box.

> look (x3)   pick   fill   ~~take~~   try   run   give   get

1 *Take* **off** your hat and coat and come in and sit down. It's freezing outside.
2 Can you help me _____ **for** my phone. I can't find it anywhere!
3 Could I _____ **on** this dress in a size 10, please?
4 My boss is great. I _____ **on** really well **with** her.
5 Can you _____ **after** my cat while I'm on holiday?
6 Don't drop your litter on the floor! _____ it **up**!
7 'Who won the Nobel Peace Prize?'
 'I don't know, I'll _____ it **up** on Google.'
8 We've _____ **out of** milk. Can you get some from the shops?
9 I'm trying to _____ **up** smoking – it's really hard!
10 You need to _____ **in** this form and sign it at the bottom.

2 Complete the sentences with a particle from the box.

> back   away   down (x2)   around   up (~~x2~~)   out (x3)

1 Joseph! Wake *up*! It's time for school!
2 Turn _____ the TV! It's too loud!
3 Did you know that Eric's going _____ with a girl at university?
4 I'm going to take this jumper _____ to the shop. It's too big!
5 Your hair looks lovely. Turn _____ so I can see it from the back.
6 There's a car coming! Look _____! It's going to hit you!
7 I live in London, but I grew _____ in Liverpool.
8 I don't know why Freya and Millie are best friends, they're always falling _____!
9 I'm really tired. I'm going to lie _____ for half an hour.
10 That's last week's Sunday paper. You can throw it _____.

🔊 **5.6** Listen and check.

3 Look at the picture. How many phrasal verbs from **1** and **2** can you see?

The verb *get*

> The verb *get* has many different meanings. Look at these lines from the reading text on page 35.
>
> *An uncle managed to get them on a plane …*
> *Finally, they got to England …*

4 What does *get* mean in these sentences? Write a word from the box.

> arrive home   receive   become   earn   ~~find~~
> leave   arrive

1 He *got* a job in an office.
 get = *find*
2 What did you *get* for your birthday?
 get = _____
3 What time does your train *get in*?
 get in = _____
4 I keep forgetting things. I'm *getting* old.
 get = _____
5 I *get* £2,000 a month.
 get = _____
6 You need to *get off* the bus at the Town Hall.
 get off = _____
7 What time did you *get in* last night?
 get in = _____

Everyday English
Expressing doubt and certainty

Underline the correct phrases in the conversation.

A Do you think Colin will pass his driving test?

B Mmm … he might do, but I ¹*doubt / know* he will. He's not a very good driver.

A He's a terrible driver! He ²*might not / definitely won't* pass. ³*Not / No* a chance!

B ⁴*Isn't he taking / Won't he take* his fifth test tomorrow?

A Yes … You ⁵*might be / 're definitely* right. I know he took the test three times last year!

B When's your test?

A I ⁶*doubt it / 'm not sure*. I'm still waiting to get a date, hopefully next month. Did you pass first time?

B ⁷*Of course! / Definitely I did!* It was easy. You'll ⁸*definitely / might* pass. You're an excellent driver.

A Hmm … ⁹*I'm not sure. / No chance*. I'm nervous because you never know what might happen during the test. ¹⁰*Anything's possible. / Not a chance.*

B You'll be fine.

A I hope so!

🔊 **5.7** Listen and check.

➡ Go online for more skills and language practice.

REVIEW
Grammar

1 Underline the correct form of the verb.

1 **A** Why are you working so hard these days?
   B Because *I'll buy / I'm going to buy* a house, so I need *to save / saving* as much as I can.

2 **A** Don't buy chocolates for Joanne's birthday. She's on a diet.
   B OK. I *'ll get / 'm getting* her some flowers.

3 **A** Mum, can you *drive / driving* me to Kevin's house?
   B Sorry, love. I'm really busy. Ask Dad. I'm sure he*'ll take / 's going to take* you.

4 **A** Why have you got so many stamps?
   B Because *I'll post / I'm going to post* my Christmas cards.

5 **A** What *will you do / are you doing* this afternoon?
   B I'm thinking of *go / going* to the cinema.

6 **A** Oh no! I've spilt my tea!
   B Don't worry, *I'm going to clean / I'll clean* it up.

7 **A** Whose wedding *are you going / will you go* to?
   B My brother's.

8 **A** I'm looking forward to *have / having* a lie-in on Sunday.
   B Me too! I'd like *to sleep / sleeping* until midday.

🔊 **5.8** Listen and check.

Vocabulary

2 Match the sentence halves.

A		B	
1	I **put**	a ☐	**down** on the sofa and watch TV.
2	Can I **try**	b ☐	**on** the light? It's really dark in here.
3	Who's going to **look**	c ☐	**off** your coat and sit by the fire.
4	You look cold! Come in. **Take**	d ☐	**after** the children while you're away?
5	Can you **turn**	e ☐	**on** this dress, please?
6	I'm really tired. I think I'll **lie**	f ☐	**down** my phone and now I can't find it!

➡ Go online to Check your progress.

Unit 5 • The future's in your hands

6 History repeats itself

- Present Perfect
- never, already, just, yet
- for, since, and ago
- Present Perfect and Past Simple
- Word endings
- Agree with me!

Grammar
Present Perfect

Positive and negative

1 Read about **Sabine Caron**. Complete the text with a verb from the box in the Present Perfect.

be	climb	have	meet	not live	ride
see	travel	not travel	start	~~work~~	write

2 Complete what Sabine says.

1 I **'ve been** to a great many countries in my life.
2 I've been to the Arctic, but I _____ _____ to the Antarctic.
3 Jean-Luc and I _____ married for many years.
4 We _____ in the US for quite a few years now.
5 We _____ never _____ dinner with the US President.
6 Our son _____ recently _____ work for a French travel magazine.

Sabine Caron
Foreign correspondent and keen traveller

Sabine Caron is French, but she now lives in the US. She's 60 years old, and she's still as active as ever. She [1] **has worked** for the newspaper *La Journal Amérique* for over ten years, as their foreign correspondent. She [2] _____ widely in Africa, the Middle East and Asia, but she [3] _____ much in Latin America yet. She [4] _____ many famous world leaders, including Nelson Mandela and three US presidents. She and her husband, the writer Jean-Luc Caron, are good friends of the French President – they [5] _____ dinner together many times, both in Paris and New York.

Her passion is travel. She [6] _____ Mount Kilimanjaro in Tanzania, she [7] _____ the Northern Lights in Alaska, and she [8] _____ a bike along the Great Wall of China. She [9] _____ a number of books about her experiences. Her book about walking in the Arctic, *Alone Again*, won an award in 2010.

She [10] _____ married to Jean-Luc for nearly 40 years. They [11] _____ in France since 2009, but they often visit their son, Leon, and his family there. Leon is following in his parents' footsteps. He's a journalist and [12] _____ just _____ work for the French magazine, *Condé Nast Traveler*.

Questions and short answers

3 You are interviewing Sabine. Complete the questions.
1 'How long _____ you _____ for the *La Journal Amérique*?'
  'For over ten years.'
2 'Which famous people _____ you _____?'
  'Nelson Mandela and the last three US presidents.'
3 '_____ you ever _____ dinner with the US President?'
  'No, I haven't! But I have with the French President.'
4 'How many books _____ you _____?'
  'Four. They're all about places I've been to.'
5 'How long _____ you _____ married to Jean-Luc?'
  'Nearly 40 years.'

4 Complete the short answers about Sabine and Jean-Luc.
1 'Has she been to China?'
  'Yes, _____.'
2 'Has she ever been to Brazil?'
  'No, _____, but she's hoping to go soon.'
3 'Has she been married more than once?'
  'No, _____. Jean-Luc is the love of her life!'
4 'Have she and Jean-Luc visited their son recently?'
  'Yes, _____. They went to Paris last month.'
5 'Has she had a good life?'
  'Yes, _____. It's been a really exciting life.'

🔊 **6.1** Listen and check.

never*, *already*, *just*, *yet

5 Put *never*, *already*, *just*, or *yet* in the right place in B's lines.
1 **A** There's a good film on at the cinema. Would you like to see it?
  B That's a nice idea, but I've seen it.
2 **A** You look awful! What's the matter?
  B I've had the most terrible news!
3 **A** Where's my white T-shirt?
  B I haven't washed it. Sorry.
4 **A** Istanbul is just amazing, isn't it?
  B I don't know. I've been there.
5 **A** Don't forget to phone Tony about Saturday.
  B I've spoken to him. He knows all about it.

🔊 **6.2** Listen and check.

for*, *since*, and *ago

6 Complete the sentences with *for*, *since*, or *ago*.
1 I've known Justin _____ we were at school together.
2 We met 20 years _____.
3 Where have you been? I haven't seen you _____ ages!
4 I haven't played tennis _____ a while.
5 I've been on a diet _____ March.
6 Once upon a time, a long time _____, there was a sad princess.

7 Write the correct answer, **a** or **b**.
1 I've been a student of English ____.
  a since three years   **b** for three years
2 How long ____ Peter?
  a have you known   **b** do you know
3 The last time I had a holiday was ____.
  a for a year   **b** a year ago
4 I lived with my parents ____.
  a until I was 16   **b** since I was a child
5 I've lived with my parents ____.
  a ten years ago   **b** all my life
6 I haven't had anything to eat ____.
  a ten hours ago   **b** since breakfast

Unit 6 • History repeats itself   39

Present Perfect and Past Simple

8 Which sentence, **a** or **b** means that Paulo still works as a waiter?
   a Paulo worked as a waiter for two months.
   b Paulo's worked as a waiter for two months.

9 Rewrite the sentences using the Past Simple and the time expression in brackets.
   1 I've already seen that film. (yesterday)
      I saw it yesterday.
   2 We've arrived in Moscow. (at six o'clock)
      We _____ here _____.
   3 She's bought a new bag. (last week)
      She _____ it _____.
   4 Damien's written a novel. (two years ago)
      He _____ it _____.
   5 They've been to Japan before. (in 2014)
      They _____ there _____.
   6 She's just begun learning French. (after her holiday in Nice)
      She _____.
   7 I've lost my phone. (last night)
      I _____ it _____.
   8 We've lived in New York. (when we were first married)
      We _____ there _____.
   9 I've worked in Italy. (from 2011 to 2018)
      I _____ in Rome _____.
   10 We've already had dinner. (before we left home)
      We _____ a curry _____.

10 Correct the mistakes in these sentences.
   1 I haven't seen that new film already.
   2 Jim hasn't yet retired.
   3 He works in the same school for 20 years.
   4 I have studied at this school for September.
   5 My grandfather died since ten years.
   6 He has lived in London until he died last year.
   7 Dave's not here. He's been to Spain on holiday.
   8 You look suntanned! Where have you gone?
   9 I can't believe I've left school ten years ago.
   10 I haven't spoken to Alice since months.

11 Put the verbs in the correct tense, Past Simple or Present Perfect.

1 **A** Who are the people in the photo?
   B They're my cousins in Australia. *Their* mum is *my* mum's big sister.
   A Oh! ¹_____ they _____ (*be*) there long?
   B Yeah! For years. They ² _____ (*go*) before I was born.
   A So, ³ _____ you _____ (*ever, meet*) them?
   B Yeah! Once! They ⁴ _____ (*come*) over to England when I was about five – but I can't remember much about it.
   A ⁵ _____ your mum _____ (*ever, visit*) them?
   B Yeah, she ⁶ _____ (*fly*) over to Sydney two years ago when my aunt was ill.
   A Is your aunt OK now?
   B She's fine. I'd love to visit them one day!

2 **A** Jake, ¹ _____ you _____ (*ever, live*) on your own?
   J Yes, of course I have!
   A When ² _____ you _____ (*do*) that?
   J When I was studying in Edinburgh. I ³ _____ (*have*) my own flat there. Why?
   A Well, I'm going to work in Spain next year, and I'm a bit worried. I ⁴ _____ (*always, live*) at home. I ⁵ _____ (*never even, cook*) a meal for myself!
   J Don't worry! You'll learn.

3 **A** Hey, Beth! It's been ages! When do you start your new job?
   B I ¹ _____ (*already, start*). I ² _____ (*start*) a week ago in fact.
   A So, how's it going? ³ _____ you _____ (*meet*) your new boss yet?
   B No, I ⁴ _____! She ⁵ _____ (*be*) abroad at a conference. She ⁶ _____ (*get back*) last night, so I'll meet her today.
   A And do you like the work so far?
   B It's early days. I ⁷ _____ (*not decide*) yet.
   A Well, good luck! Let me know how it goes!

🔊 **6.3** Listen and check.

The Koch family

12 Read the article about **Jim Koch**. Answer the questions.
1. What was his family's business?
2. Why did his father not want him to continue in it?
3. What is the biggest lesson Jim has learned?

13 Read the article again. Underline the correct tense – Past Simple, Past Continuous or Present Perfect.

14 Which of these sentences are true (✓) or false (✗)? Correct the false ones.
1. ☐ The family business has always been successful.
2. ☐ Jim went to one of the best American universities.
3. ☐ Jim named the beer after his great-great-grandfather.
4. ☐ Americans were growing tired of the beer produced by the big beer companies.
5. ☐ Jim's company has become more successful than he imagined.
6. ☐ He has always believed that that happiness comes from making money.

Family fortunes
from failure to success!

Jim Koch giving a tour of the brewery

The Koch family ¹ *has brewed* / *brewed* beer for six generations, but when Jim Koch wanted to continue the family tradition, his father ² *thought* / *was thinking* it was a very bad idea. He said, 'Jim, you ³ *did* / *have done* some dumb things in your life, but this is the dumbest.'

This was 1984, the beer industry in America was in a bad way and the family business ⁴ *has suffered* / *was suffering*. At that time, Harvard-graduate Jim ⁵ *was earning* / *has earned* a high salary as a business consultant, but he ⁶ *wasn't enjoying* / *hasn't enjoyed* it. So, despite his father's disapproval, he ⁷ *left* / *has left* his job and decided to rebuild the family brewery business. He ⁸ *didn't want* / *wasn't wanting* to compete with the big breweries, he just wanted to make good quality, traditionally brewed beer.

Jim ⁹ *discovered* / *has discovered* his great-great-grandfather's German beer recipe in the attic, and used it to create his first lager. He named it 'Samuel Adams', after the 18th century Boston brewer and war hero. Jim was both clever and lucky – his 'craft' quality beer ¹⁰ *hit* / *was hitting* the market at the perfect time, when Americans ¹¹ *began* / *was beginning* to grow tired of mass produced beer. Twenty years later, in 2004, Jim's company was worth $70 million!

Since then the popularity of 'craft' beer ¹² *has continued* / *continued* to grow. There are now more than 5,000 craft breweries in the US, worth $23.5 billion! Jim's company ¹³ *became* / *has become* a billion-dollar business – it sells three to four billion barrels of beer a year. He can't believe how much money he ¹⁴ *made* / *has made* already. He says, 'My plan was to get about a million dollars a year in sales.'

Over the years Jim ¹⁵ *was learning* / *has learned* many lessons about life, but he says the biggest one is 'Do what makes you happy rather than what's going to make you rich.'

Vocabulary
Word endings

1 Complete the tables.

1

Noun	Adjective
1 success	*successful*
2	expensive
3 responsibility	
4	famous
5 danger	
6	happy
7 music	
8	healthy

2

Noun	Verb
1 success	*succeed*
2	compete
3 invitation	
4	practise
5 collection	
6	discover
7 comparison	
8	decide

3

Noun (thing)	Noun (person)
1 history	historian
2 photograph	
3 politics	
4 art	
5 psychology	
6 science	
7 invention	
8 music	

2 Complete the sentences with a word from the charts.
1. Sigmund Freud was a famous _____.
2. Mozart showed great _____ talent from an early age.
3. Did you hear the Prime Minister's speech? I think all _____ lie!
4. If at first you don't _____, try, try again.
5. Alexander Fleming's _____ of penicillin has saved many lives.
6. The computer _____ Tim Berners-Lee invented the World Wide Web.
7. My son came first in his school spelling _____. I'm very proud.
8. Your English pronunciation has really improved – you see _____ makes perfect!

Word stress

3 Write the words in the box under the correct stress pattern in the table.

~~successful~~	invite	invitation	musical
artist	competition	famous	happiness
collection	decision	photograph	succeed
politician	discuss	danger	

1 ●●	2 ●●	3 ●●●
		successful

4 ●●●	5 ●●●●

🔊 6.4 Listen, check, and repeat.

Everyday English
Agree with me!

1 Match a sentence in **A** with a question tag in **B**.

A	B
1 That was a great meal,	didn't we?
2 This isn't the best restaurant in town,	didn't they?
3 We come here a lot,	haven't we?
4 We came here for Tina's birthday,	isn't it?
5 Everyone had a great time,	wasn't it?
6 You like the Italian restaurant best,	don't we?
7 The Indian in the High Street's very good,	don't you?
8 We've had a lovely evening,	is it?

2 Match the answers in **C** with a sentence in **1**.

C
a It's certainly not my favourite.
b Yes, we do. Probably because it's so cheap.
c Well, it was OK, but I've had better.
d We did. That was a good evening.
e Yes, I do. Their pizzas are fabulous.
f They did. The food wasn't great, but it didn't matter.
g It's been really nice – but let's go to the Italian next time.
h It's OK, but I'm not too keen on spicy food.

🔊 **6.5** Listen and check.

Giles Coren, restaurant critic

📱 **Go online** for more skills and language practice.

REVIEW
Grammar

1 Complete **B**'s answers using a verb from the box in the Present Perfect.

| finish | play | have | speak | eat | try | take |

1 **A** Would you like a cup of coffee?
   B No, thanks. I _____ already _____ two cups.
2 **A** Can you play chess?
   B Yes, but I _____ for years!
3 **A** How's your sister these days?
   B I don't know. I _____ to her for weeks.
4 **A** What did you think of that book?
   B I'll tell you later. I _____ reading it yet.
5 **A** Do you like Thai food?
   B I've no idea. I _____ never _____ it.
6 **A** Are you hungry?
   B I'm starving! I _____ anything all day!
7 **A** Mmm! That cake looks good! Can I have some?
   B Not yet. I _____ only just _____ it out of the oven.

2 Choose the correct answer about **Giles Coren**, the writer and restaurant critic.

1 Giles Coren ____ in London.
   a has lived   **b** lived   **c** lives
2 He ____ to Oxford University.
   a has gone   **b** goes   **c** went
3 He's been restaurant critic for *The Times* newspaper ____ 1993.
   a for   **b** since   **c** last
4 He ____ in more than 10,000 restaurants.
   a eats   **b** has eaten   **c** was eating
5 He is often very rude, but then says that he ____.
   a only joked   **b** has only joked   **c** was only joking
6 He won *Restaurant Writer of the Year* award ____ 2016.
   a since   **b** on   **c** in
7 His wife is also a writer. They ____ two children.
   a got   **b** have got   **c** had
8 His sister, Victoria, ____ for *The Observer* newspaper.
   a writes   **b** wrote   **c** was writing
9 She also plays poker. She ____ over $1 million already.
   a wins   **b** has won   **c** won
10 Giles' father was a writer, too. He died ____.
   a several years ago   **b** since several years
   c for several years

📱 **Go online** to Check your progress.

Unit 6 • History repeats itself

7 Simply the best

- What's it like?
- Comparatives and superlatives
- Prepositions
- Synonyms and antonyms
- What's on?

Grammar
What's it like?

1 You have a friend who's living in Brazil. Ask questions about the country using *What … like?*

1 the weather
   What's the weather like?

2 the food
   _____

3 the people
   _____

4 Rio de Janeiro
   _____

5 the nightlife
   _____

6 the beaches
   _____

2 Match a question in exercise **1** with an answer.

a [3] They're lovely. Really kind and friendly.
b [ ] It's warm all year round. Even in the winter it usually doesn't go below 18°C.
c [ ] They're beautiful with lovely soft white sand. Copacabana's my favourite.
d [ ] It's an amazing city. The views from Sugarloaf Mountain are spectacular.
e [ ] It's delicious – lots of beef, pork, and beans.
f [ ] It's so exciting. You can party all night in the cocktail bars and nightclubs.

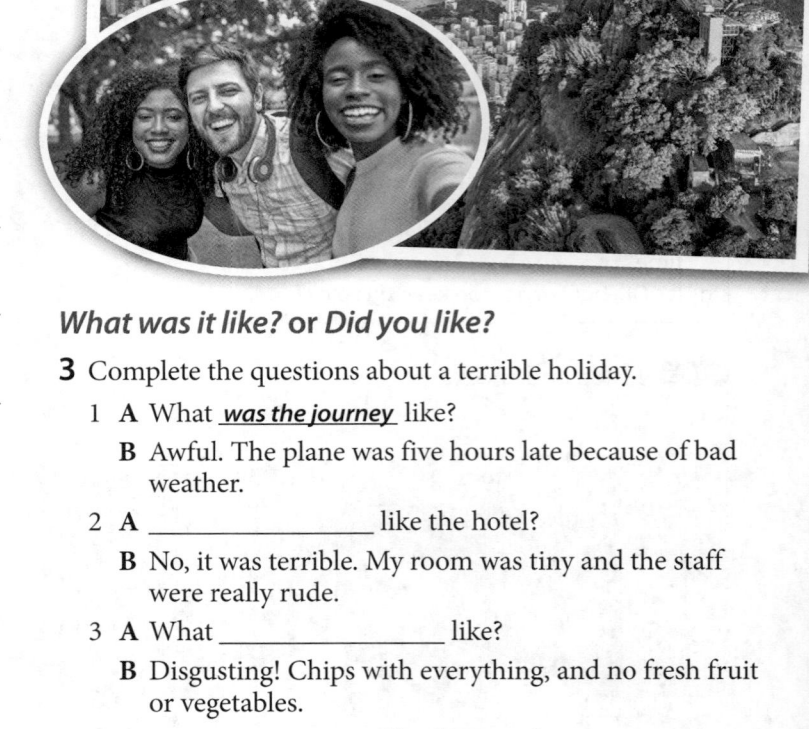

🔊 **7.1** Listen and check.

What was it like? or Did you like?

3 Complete the questions about a terrible holiday.

1 **A** What _was the journey_ like?
   B Awful. The plane was five hours late because of bad weather.
2 **A** _____ like the hotel?
   B No, it was terrible. My room was tiny and the staff were really rude.
3 **A** What _____ like?
   B Disgusting! Chips with everything, and no fresh fruit or vegetables.
4 **A** _____ like the town?
   B No, it was boring. There was nothing to do there.
5 **A** What _____ like?
   B It rained every day, apart from the day I came home!

🔊 **7.2** Listen and check.

44 Unit 7 · Simply the best

Comparing two people

4 Two of the answers to each question are correct. Tick (✓) the correct answers.

1 'What does Jaco look like?'
   a ☐ 'He's taller than me! And quite good-looking.'
   b ☐ 'He's a really nice guy. I like him a lot.'
   c ☐ 'He's tall and slim, with short blond hair.'

2 'What's Jaco like?'
   a ☐ 'He's a great guy, really interesting.'
   b ☐ 'He's the funniest guy I know. I like him a lot.'
   c ☐ 'He likes playing football and travelling.'

3 'Do you like Jaco?'
   a ☐ 'Yes, he's one of my best friends!'
   b ☐ 'I'm not like Jaco at all!'
   c ☐ 'Yes, of course! Everybody loves Jaco!'

4 'What does Jaco like?'
   a ☐ 'He's very caring. He always helps his friends.'
   b ☐ 'He loves football and visiting other countries.'
   c ☐ 'He eats a lot of Indian food. The spicier the better!'

5 Write questions about Rita.

1 '**What does Rita look like**_____?'
   'She's quite tall, pretty, and she's got long blonde hair.'
2 '_____?'
   'She's a lovely person. She's really kind.'
3 '_____?'
   'Playing tennis, going to the gym and cooking.'
4 '_____?'
   'Yes, I do. She's one of the kindest people I know.'

6 Look at the information about Jaco and Rita. Complete the sentences.

1 Jaco _is younger than_ Rita.
2 _____ is friendlier than _____.
3 Jaco is a lot _____ than Rita.
4 _____ is richer than _____.
5 _____ earns more _____.
6 Rita has a much _____.
7 _____ is bigger _____.
8 Rita's house was _____.
9 Jaco's house is _____ modern _____.

Rita		Jaco
Personal		
24	1 age	22
✓✓✓✓	2 friendly	✓✓✓
✓✓✓	3 confident	✓✓✓✓✓
Wealth and job		
has £100,000	4 money	has £50,000
£80,000	5 salary	£30,000
✓✓✓✓✓	6 interesting job	✓✓
House		
230m²	7 size	140m²
£450,000	8 price	£180,000
1898	9 date built	2017

Unit 7 • Simply the best

as … as

7 Rewrite the sentences using *as … as* or *not as … as*.

1. Her work is good. And my work is also good.
   Her work is **as good as** mine.
2. Scotland is colder than England.
   England isn't _____ Scotland.
3. Bill's taller than me.
   I'm _____ Bill.
4. My car cost £60,000. Her car also cost £60,000.
   Her car was _____ mine.
5. Jane's house is older than Harry's.
   Jane's house _____ modern _____ Harry's.
6. Your daughter isn't shorter than you any more!
   Your daughter is _____ you now!

Superlatives

8 Write sentences to disagree with these sentences. Use the opposite adjective in its superlative form.

1. Ethan is the noisiest boy in the group.
   No, he isn't! He's the quietest.
2. She bought the cheapest bag in the shop.
   _____
3. This is the easiest exercise in the book.
   _____
4. This is the most beautiful building I've ever seen.
   _____
5. Jim is the meanest person I know.
   _____
6. The Olive Tree is the best restaurant in town.
   _____

Prepositions

9 Match a sentence beginning in **A** with a preposition in **B** and an ending in **C**.

A	B	C
1 It's the tallest	as	her brothers.
2 Yours is the same	than	the others.
3 She's younger	like	his father.
4 He looks	in	mine.
5 They're different	from	the world.

Comparatives and superlatives

10 Correct the sentences.

1. He's more older than he looks.
2. Jessica's as tall than her mother.
3. London is more expensive that Vienna.
4. Oxford is one of oldest universities in Europe.
5. He isn't as intelligent than his sister.
6. This is more hard than I expected.
7. Who is the most rich man in the world?
8. Everything is more cheap in my country.
9. The great white shark is the more dangerous shark in the world.
10. Your idea is much more good than mine.

How old am I?

11 Read the text and answer the questions.

I have two sisters, Jenny and Samantha, and two brothers, Henry and Chris.

Jenny is 20. Samantha is six years younger than Jenny, and two years older than Chris. Chris is four years younger than me, and he is eight years younger than Henry.

Me

Jenny Samantha Henry Chris

1. How old am I?
   _____
2. Who is the youngest in the family?
   _____
3. How old is Samantha?
   _____
4. Is Samantha older than me?
   _____
5. Am I the oldest of the children?
   _____
6. How old are the twins?
   _____

The youngest girl to conquer Everest

12 Write the comparative or superlative form of the adjective in brackets.

Malavath Poorna
Youngest teen to climb Mount Everest

Malavath Poorna was only 13 years old when she climbed Mount Everest. She is the ¹ *youngest* (*young*) girl ever to reach the summit of the world's ² _____ (*high*) mountain – an incredible achievement for the daughter of a farm worker from India. She is now a national celebrity, and there is a film about her adventures.

From the bottom to the top!

Malavath attended a school for underprivileged* children. The secretary of the school, Dr R.S. Praveen Kumar, had a dream. He believed that by training a young person to climb Everest, he could show India's ³ _____ (*poor*) citizens that there are opportunities for everyone. By making a farmer's daughter into one of India's ⁴ _____ (*good*) climbers, he showed that anything was possible.

Malavath was ⁵ _____ (*good*) at sports than a lot of the other students, and ⁶ _____ (*fit*) too, so she was one of two students chosen for the Everest climb, which involved ice and snow training. She knew nothing about climbing before she began the training, and was amazed to learn that she was going to climb the ⁷ _____ (*famous*) mountain in the world. The training was a lot ⁸ _____ (*hard*) than she expected.

The ⁹ _____ (*frightening*) moment for Malavath was when they found six dead bodies. 'I was scared,' she says, but then she remembered her school motto: *The sky is the limit!* 'I wanted to prove that girls could do anything.'

Dreaming big

Since climbing Everest, Malavath has also climbed Africa's ¹⁰ _____ (*tall*) mountain, Mount Kilimanjaro in Tanzania. She's now working hard for her exams, because she wants to join the Indian Police Service. She continues to encourage Indian girls to 'dream big', and tells them they can be as good as the boys – or even ¹¹ _____ (*good*)!

The film about Malavath's journey to Everest is called *Poorna*. The film's director, Rahul Bose, said, 'Malavath Poorna is the ¹² _____ (*remarkable*) person I have ever met.'

> **underprivileged** having less money and fewer opportunities than most people in society

13 Are the sentences true (✓) or false (✗)? Correct the false sentences.

1 ☐ Malavath's school was for some of the poorest families in India.
2 ☐ Malavath was chosen to climb Everest because she was the youngest in her class.
3 ☐ She was a more experienced climber than the other students in the school.
4 ☐ The training wasn't as hard as she expected.
5 ☐ The worst part of the climb was seeing climbers who never came back from the mountain.
6 ☐ After Everest, Malavath climbed the tallest mountain in Europe.
7 ☐ Malavath believes that girls can sometimes do better than boys.
8 ☐ The director of *Poorna* thinks that Malavath is more talented than most young people.

Vocabulary
Synonyms and antonyms

1 Match an adjective in **A** with a synonym in **B**.

A	B
1 difficult	☐ a pleased
2 correct	☐ b right
3 happy	☐ c hard
4 clever	☐ d frightened
5 scared	☐ e intelligent
6 unusual	☐ f well-known
7 big	☐ g strange
8 famous	☐ h good-looking
9 handsome	☐ i large
10 lovely	☐ j wonderful

2 Complete the conversations with a synonym from **1**.

I'm really scared of mice.
I'm frightened of them, too.

1 'This exercise is really hard.'
  'I know, it's too _____ for me.'
2 'Harry's such a handsome young man.'
  'I wish I was as _____ as him!'
3 'Richard is really intelligent.'
  'Yes, he's so _____. He gets 100% in everything!'
4 'It's strange weather for this time of year.'
  'Yes, it is _____. We never get snow in May!'
5 'I'm not very pleased with my new laptop.'
  'Well, if you're not _____ with it, you should take it back to the shop.'
6 'We had a lovely time in Florence last week.'
  'Mmm, I've heard Tuscany is _____ this time of year.'

🔊 7.3 Listen and check.

3 Complete the table with the words in the box.

| cheap wrong quiet ~~rude~~ dirty stupid |
| miserable boring |

Adjective	Antonym
1 polite	*rude*
2 clean	
3 expensive	
4 happy	
5 interesting	
6 correct	
7 intelligent	
8 noisy	

4 Complete the sentences with a word from **3**.

1 Some people are so rude! You should always be _____ to others.
2 This glass is dirty! Could you give me a _____ one, please?
3 Fran thought the film was interesting, but I thought it was _____.
4 I thought my answer was wrong, but the teacher said it was _____.
5 Why are the children so quiet? They're usually very _____.
6 I'm always _____ on Monday, but then I'm really happy on Friday.
7 Einstein was really intelligent. I'm so _____ compared to him.
8 Dubai is so expensive. Nothing is _____!

Palm Islands, Dubai

48 Unit 7 • Simply the best

Everyday English
What's on?

Underline the correct words in the conversation.

A What ¹*shall / may* we do today? The weather is awful!

B How ²*about / around* going to the cinema? There's that new Hugh Jackman film on.

A Hmm. I don't really ³*would like / feel like* seeing a film.

B OK. ⁴*Would / Do* you like to go to the art gallery in Hyde Park?

A That ⁵*feels / sounds* like a good idea. ⁶*What's on? / Where's it on?*

B A photography exhibition.

A Oh, ⁷*good / not my kind of thing*. I love photography. What's the subject?

B I'm not absolutely sure, but I think it's nature photography.

A Great! I'm really interested in that. We can have lunch at Harrods and get the bus to Hyde Park. What time does the gallery ⁸*open / close*?

B Not until four o'clock, so we've got plenty of time.

A ⁹*How much is it? / Is it expensive to get in?*

B No, it's free, but we need to book. I'll ring now!

A Free! That's good! More to spend on lunch!

🔊 **7.4** Listen and check.

📲 Go online for more skills and language practice.

REVIEW
Grammar

1 Complete the sentences with the comparative or superlative form of the adjective in brackets.
1. Today is much _____ (*cold*) than yesterday.
2. Grace is _____ (*intelligent*) in the class.
3. Madrid is _____ (*hot*) than London.
4. I got _____ (*bad*) grade in the class.
5. Spanish is _____ (*easy*) to learn than Chinese.
6. Shanghai is _____ (*modern*) than Singapore.
7. Your car is much _____ (*expensive*) than mine.
8. Charles de Gaulle is one of _____ (*busy*) airports in the world.

Vocabulary

2 Choose the correct answer.
1. Are you ____ of spiders?
   a scared   **b** frightening
2. Well done! You've got all your spellings ____.
   a right   **b** good
3. J.K.Rowling is rich, but she gives a lot of money to charity. She's a very ____ woman.
   a polite   **b** generous
4. I ____ my sister. We both have brown eyes and short brown hair.
   a look like   **b** like
5. 'What's your teacher ____?'
   'She's really good. I'm learning a lot.'
   a look like   **b** like
6. 'Do you like Fiona?'
   '____'
   a She's very intelligent.   **b** She's OK.
7. 'What does your mum like?'
   '____'
   a Gardening and walking.   **b** Really kind.
8. Carol is a very ____ person. I could talk to her all day.
   a happy   **b** interesting

📲 Go online to Check your progress.

Unit 7 • Simply the best   49

8 Living dangerously

- *have to* – present and past obligation
- *must*
- *should*
- Not a thing to wear!
- At the doctor's

Grammar *have to*

Present obligation – *have to/don't have to*

1 **Sammy** is a top London chef, and a boxer in his free time. Complete the interview using the lines a–k.

a don't have to be
b Do you have to go
c has to come
d you have to try
e ~~do you have to be~~
f have to work
g have to make sure
h doesn't have to be
i don't have to work
j have to have
k do you have to do

The boxing chef

I Sammy, what kind of person ¹ _e_ to become a successful chef?

S Well, number one, you ² ___ a passion for cooking – food ³ ___ first in your life!

I That can't be easy for your family!

S No, it isn't, but Olivia, my wife, is very understanding.

I What sort of training ⁴ ___ to become a chef? ⁵ ___ to college?

S Most people go to catering college, and then you ⁶ ___ as an apprentice in a big kitchen. But it ⁷ ___ in a restaurant. My first job was cooking at my local hospital.

I Really! And now you're a head chef at a Michelin star restaurant!

S Yes, but I also worked in restaurants in Spain and France. You ⁸ ___ abroad, but it helps.

I So, do you get much free time?

S Well, you ⁹ ___ you take enough time off. Stress is a real problem for chefs – it's one of the most dangerous professions for mental health problems.

I Really? And what do you do in your free time?

S I'm a boxer, so when I ¹⁰ ___ at the restaurant, I often train at the gym. My grandfather and father were both professional boxers – they can't believe I'm a chef!

I Well, boxing doesn't seem a very good way to get away from the stress and danger! I imagine ¹¹ ___ hard not to get injured!

S Yes, I don't want to get too many black eyes. It doesn't look very good at the restaurant!

2 Complete the questions using *have to*.

1 'What **do** you **have to** have a passion for to be a good chef?'
  'Cooking!'

2 'What sort of college _____ chefs _____ go to?'
  'A catering college.'

3 '_____ you _____ work abroad to be a successful chef?'
  'No, but it helps.'

4 'What does Sammy do when he _____ be at the restaurant?'
  'He trains at the gym.'

5 'Why _____ he _____ try hard not to get a black eye?'
  'Because it doesn't look good at the restaurant!'

🔊 **8.1** Listen and check.

50 Unit 8 • Living dangerously

Past obligation – had to/didn't have to

3 Complete the lines in the conversation between Sammy and his grandfather with *had to* or *didn't have to*.

G Hi, Sammy. Are you still working hard at that expensive restaurant of yours?

S Yes, Grandad. I'm working very hard.

G Well, not as hard as I did at your age. I ¹_____ work ten hours a day at the car factory, and I ²_____ train for my boxing every day, too.

S But you ³_____ work until midnight, Grandad, like I do. And I sometimes have to get up at 5.00 a.m. to go to the fish market.

G I ⁴_____ get up at 5.00 when I was ten, to light the fire in the kitchen! You ⁵_____ light fires when you were ten.

S No, but I ⁶_____ get up at 6.00 to deliver newspapers.

G Hmm! You had it easy! Now, boxing, that is hard training. How often are you at the boxing club?

S I try and go twice a week, but I just don't have the time. You ⁷_____ work 18-hour days! Your life was hard, but simpler.

G Yes, it was simpler. For a start, we ⁸_____ do all this online stuff. I feel sorry for younger people today – you're always busy on your phones! I had work and boxing, and then it was time for the pub – until I met your grandma!

S Oh, Grandad! You ⁹_____ get married to Grandma – and she says you ¹⁰_____ ask her five times before she said yes!

G OK, OK. Well, she was the loveliest girl on our street – and still is!

🔊 **8.2** Listen and check.

Possession and obligation

4 Does *have* mean possession (P) or obligation (O) in these sentences? Write **P** or **O**.

1 He has a really expensive car. **P**
2 She has to walk the dog twice a day. **O**
3 How many spellings do we have to learn? ____
4 When can we have a coffee break? ____
5 I have two brothers and a sister. ____
6 I have to do so much work before tomorrow. ____
7 How many hours a day did she have to train? ____
8 Did she have a lot of homework? ____

must

5 Complete the sentences with *must* and a verb in the box.

| tidy | ~~send~~ | meet | reply | drive | text | stay |

1 It's my grandmother's 80th birthday next week. I **must send** her a birthday card.
2 The flat is such a mess! I _____ it up before my parents visit tomorrow.
3 You _____ at the Old Parsonage when you go to Oxford. It's the best hotel in the city.
4 I _____ Miles to tell him what time the party starts.
5 You can borrow my car, but you _____ carefully.
6 I _____ to all my emails! I have so many!
7 Julie and Mark are a lovely couple. You _____ them. You'll really get on well.

mustn't or don't have to?

6 **EXTENSION** Complete the sentences with *mustn't* or *don't/doesn't have to*.

1 You _____ drive too fast. It's dangerous.
2 You _____ eat it if you don't like it.
3 Travelling on the underground is free if you're under 16. You _____ pay.
4 Theo has flu. The doctor says he _____ go to work.
5 Vicky _____ go to bed late. She has to get an early flight in the morning.
6 Matilda's family is really rich. She _____ work.
7 You _____ eat too much chocolate cake. You'll be sick!
8 Henry _____ go to the party if he doesn't want to.

Unit 8 • Living dangerously   51

should

7 Give advice to these people. Use *I think ... should ...* or *I don't think ... should ...* and a phrase from the box.

> go by bus instead   say sorry   go to the dentist
> ~~go to work today~~   eat so much chocolate
> stay out all night   take it back to the shop

1 Ella's got a bad cold.
   I don't think she should go to work today.

2 My tooth hurts.
   _____

3 Piper wants to walk to work, but it's raining heavily.
   _____

4 Adrian and Jason are only 16, but they want to go to an all-night party.
   _____

5 Elijah's crying because I pushed him. It was a mistake.
   _____

6 This watch isn't working. I only bought it last week!
   _____

7 I'm so fat! My jeans don't fit me anymore!
   _____

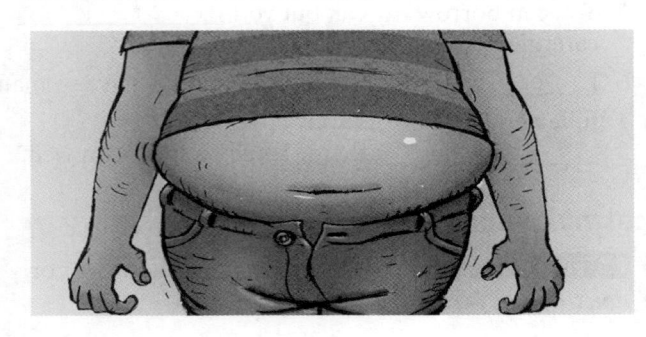

8 Ask for advice in these situations. Use *do you think ... should ...?*

1 Eddie has asked me to marry him.
   What do you think I should say?

2 We want to go to the cinema.
   Which film _____ ?

3 I want to go away for the weekend.
   Where _____ ?

4 We're going to have a barbecue for 20 people.
   How many sausages _____ ?

5 Stewart's parents are coming for dinner.
   What _____ ?

should or have to

9 Complete the sentences with a form of *have to* or *should*. Make the verbs negative when necessary.

1 Your hair is too long. I think you _____ have a haircut.

2 You've always got a cough. You _____ give up smoking.

3 I'm going to bed now. I _____ get up early tomorrow.

4 I'd like to meet your new boyfriend. You _____ ask him round for a drink some time.

5 You _____ tell lies. It's wrong.

6 If you've got a ticket you _____ queue. You can go straight in.

7 In the UK you _____ drive on the left.

8 You _____ come with me. I'm happy to go on my own.

9 Kiki works too hard. I think she _____ take it easy.

10 'Do we _____ go to school today?'
   'Of course you do.'

should or must

10 Look at the instructions for London cycle couriers. Choose the correct answers.

London cycle couriers

1 You *must / mustn't* wear a helmet at all times.
2 You *must / mustn't* cycle on the pavement.
3 You *must / mustn't* stop at traffic lights.
4 You *should / shouldn't* expect drivers to drive safely.
5 You *should / shouldn't* be rude to other road users.
6 You *should / shouldn't* wear a mask when pollution levels are high.

Lucy Nicholls – City cyclist

11 Read the text about Lucy. Are these sentences true (✓) or false (✗)? Correct the false sentences.

1. ☐ Lucy has to cycle 500 miles every week.
2. ☐ As a London courier cyclist, Lucy hasn't had any accidents.
3. ☐ The courier company have to pay her when she's off work.
4. ☐ In winter, London courier cyclists should check the weather forecast every day.
5. ☐ Lucy has to spend a lot of money on warm clothes every week.
6. ☐ Lucy thinks she will stay in this job for a long time.

12 Complete the questions. Use the correct form of *have to*.

1. 'How many miles **do** cycle couriers **have to cycle** a day?'
   'Between 60 to 100 miles.'
2. 'Why _____ you _____ fearless?'
   'Because it's difficult and dangerous work.'
3. 'When _____ a courier _____ especially strong?'
   'In winter.'
4. 'What _____ couriers _____ to keep warm in winter?'
   'They have to keep cycling.'
5. 'Why _____ Lucy _____ a mask sometimes?'
   'Because of pollution.'

🔊 **8.3** Listen and check.

Lucy Nicholls Cycle courier

Lucy Nicholls has lived in London all her life, but it was only when she became a cycle courier that she really got to know the city and the dangers of city cycling.

Lucy has always loved cycling, so getting a job as a cycle courier seemed a good idea. A London courier cycles between 60 to 100 miles a day so you have to be fit.

'I knew I had to cycle a lot of miles, but I never expected to sometimes do 500 miles a week', says Lucy.

This job isn't just about being fit. You have to be fearless, too. You have to learn to understand the road and expect people to behave badly. Bicycle couriering is difficult and dangerous work.

'White van drivers are the worst', says Lucy, *'they think they don't have to follow the rules, they go through red lights and show no respect to other road users, especially couriers.'*

Taxi drivers aren't very polite either. Lucy has had to go to hospital twice because of accidents with London 'cabbies', and there's no sick pay for couriers – you only earn when you ride.

'Some taxi drivers think they own London. They should learn a few manners', says Lucy.

But it's not just the other drivers that make it a dangerous job. Pedestrians looking at their phones, huge potholes in the roads and traffic lights everywhere mean that couriers have to be on constant alert.

Then there's the winter. A courier has to be especially strong to survive the winter.

'You have to keep cycling or you freeze', says Lucy, *'your toes freeze, your fingers freeze and your joints go completely stiff. And then of course there's the London rain.'*

During the winter a London cycle courier watches the weather forecast religiously, and the weather becomes their life.

'I had to spend a whole week's earnings on a good waterproof coat, thermal gloves and a hat to keep warm', says Lucy.

There's also the air quality. The pollution in London sometimes reaches dangerous levels.

'On bad days I can feel the dirt in my lungs, and I have to wear a mask.'

So why do it?

'Despite the traffic, the pollution, the cold and the road rage*, I love it. I totally focus on my body moving with my bike. I know I will have to get another job eventually, no one can do this job for too long, but I love it for now.'

rage anger

Vocabulary
Not a thing to wear!

1 Write the words from the box under the correct heading.

> ~~shoes~~ ~~fingers~~ ~~jacket~~
> waist   ankles   socks   boots
> hoodie   pyjamas   vest
> sandals   tracksuit   slippers
> wrist   belt   shoulders   neck
> trainers   leggings   toes

1 **Parts of the body**

fingers
_____
_____
_____
_____
_____

2 **Things you wear on your body**

jacket
_____
_____
_____
_____
_____
_____

3 **Things you wear on your feet**

shoes
_____
_____
_____
_____

2 Find ten parts of the body in the wordsearch.

E	A	R	B	K	J	C	L	A	I	O	M
S	I	X	P	C	F	I	N	G	E	R	C
J	W	B	Y	H	Q	D	K	G	F	M	M
B	G	H	H	A	U	B	F	U	Y	D	Q
Z	A	M	V	N	I	S	G	D	S	K	O
W	C	F	O	D	J	M	O	U	T	H	P
A	R	M	T	M	E	I	C	S	E	N	H
L	N	C	J	S	Y	K	T	A	T	H	F
L	D	A	R	W	E	M	F	L	E	R	O
E	I	R	Y	M	Z	K	I	M	E	L	O
G	I	Q	K	B	C	L	M	G	T	O	T
W	G	Y	N	O	S	E	F	G	H	I	K

3 EXTENSION Write the body parts you use to do the activities below.

1 You use your _ears_ to listen.
2 You use your _____ to type.
3 You use your _____ to smell.
4 You use your _____ to walk.
5 You use your _____ to blink.
6 You use your _____ to kiss.
7 You use your _____ to bite.
8 You use your _____ to hug.
9 You use your _____ to kick.
10 You use your _____ to clap.

Everyday English
At the doctor's

Complete the sentences with the correct form of the verbs in the box.

| swallow | take | feel | drink | blow | ~~ache~~ | be |
| hurt | sneeze | go | sprain | | | |

1 I've got flu. My body _aches_ all over and I _____ terrible!

2 I've got a cold. I can't stop _____ and _____ my nose.

3 I've _____ my ankle. It really _____ to walk.

4 I've got food poisoning. I _____ sick three times!

5 I've got a sore throat. I can't _____ and my glands are swollen.

6 I've got diarrhoea. I have to _____ to the toilet – now!

7 It's important to _____ lots of fluids when you have a high temperature.

8 I've just had an operation. I have to _____ things easy for a couple of weeks.

REVIEW
Grammar

1 Correct the mistakes in each sentence.
 1 He hasn't to work. He's a multi-millionaire.
 2 Have you to wear a uniform for your job?
 3 I have study hard because I want to get a good job.
 4 We not have to get up early on Saturday.
 5 When I was a child, I have to help my mother with the housework.
 6 Do you have to an English lesson today?
 7 You mustn't eat the soup if you don't like it.
 8 I don't think you must marry Kevin – he doesn't love you.

2 Choose the correct answer a, b or c.
 1 I ____ wear glasses because my eyes aren't very good.
  a have   b have to   c don't have to
 2 I think Penny ____ go to bed. She looks tired.
  a should   b doesn't have to   c must
 3 We ____ go to work today because it's the weekend!
  a mustn't   b don't have to   c shouldn't
 4 Do you think I ____ wear this dress to Zoe's party?
  a have to   b must   c should
 5 I ____ stay up late. I have to get up early tomorrow.
  a mustn't   b must   c should
 6 You ____ do all your boyfriend's washing. Tell him to do it himself!
  a should   b must   c shouldn't
 7 As a child, I ____ work in my dad's shop on Saturdays because he was so busy.
  a have to   b had to   c didn't have to
 8 I ____ go to my English class today because my teacher was off sick.
  a had to   b don't have to   c didn't have to

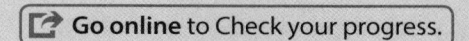

Stop and check Units 5–8

Grammar

1 Choose the correct answer.

1 Who do you _____ like? Your mother or father?
   a be
   b look
   c take
2 Lena's not looking forward _____ her exam results!
   a getting
   b to getting
   c to get
3 Let's meet again soon. I _____ give you a call sometime next week.
   a 'm going to
   b hope to
   c 'll
4 What _____ when I rang? You sounded out of breath.
   a did you do
   b were you doing
   c have you done
5 What do you want _____ for your birthday?
   a do
   b to do
   c doing
6 I'm not going to upgrade my phone _____.
   a already
   b just
   c yet
7 I'm fed up _____ having to work late every day.
   a of
   b with
   c at
8 He _____ teaching very much.
   a doesn't want
   b doesn't enjoy
   c isn't good at
9 He's a very friendly dog! How long _____ him?
   a do you have
   b did you have
   c have you had
10 My sister moved to Canada a year _____.
   a ago
   b since
   c past

11 Barbara often _____ work at weekends.
   a has to
   b must
   c should
12 She _____ wear a uniform.
   a doesn't have to
   b mustn't
   c shouldn't
13 She doesn't know if she _____ marry James or not.
   a has to
   b must
   c should
14 I've _____ met a famous person in my life.
   a ever
   b never
   c just
15 Sam was just six when his family _____ to Singapore.
   a moved
   b were moving
   c have moved
16 It's _____ film I've ever seen.
   a best
   b funniest
   c the funniest
17 I asked Ingrid what her brother was _____.
   a liking
   b like
   c liked
18 Roberto's not as much fun _____ his brother Alfonso.
   a as
   b like
   c than
19 That's _____ match I've ever seen.
   a most exciting
   b the most exciting
   c the most excited
20 There's nothing _____ than chips without salt. They're tasteless.
   a worse
   b worst
   c better

SCORE 20

Vocabulary

2 Use the clues to complete the crossword.

ACROSS

1 I don't want to talk much today – I've got a sore _____. (6)
4 'Is that restaurant good?' 'I've _____ _____. I've never eaten there'. (2,4)
9 The noun form of *happy*. (9)
11 Opposite of *polite*. (4)
12 Life was harder in the past, _____ simpler. (3)
13 You've _____ your leg. I'll take you to hospital. (6)
15 She gave _____ of the most inspirational speeches I've ever heard. (3)
16 Bindi Irwin's band was called The _____ Girls. (6)
17 Opposite of *furthest*. (7)
19 Drivers can suffer from _____ rage. (4)
20 The first Roman newspaper was written on _____. (5)
23 I need a pen to _____ _____ this form. (4, 2)
25 Mmm! I love _____ cake – it's my favourite! (9)
27 We're eating in 30 minutes. _____ patient! (2)
28 I often chat with my mum on the phone – she _____ me most days. (5)
29 You don't have to study to be a chef, but it _____. (5)
30 I'm not lucky – I've never _____ a competition. (3)
33 I don't like hats but I often wear a baseball _____. (3)
34 You can't watch TV _____ you've finished your homework. (5)
35 All archaeologists would love to _____ an ancient Egyptian tomb! (8)
36 It was a lovely day so we _____ to go for a walk on the beach. (7)

DOWN

2 A jacket with a hood is called a _____. (6)
3 He's a _____ chef – he works for a famous restaurant. (3)
4 Can we go somewhere quieter? There's too much _____ in here. (5)
5 The noun form of *destroy*. (11)
6 He's 35, but he still lives _____ home. (2)
7 Julian Lennon has _____ a children's book. (7)
8 _____ _____ the lights before you leave. (4, 3)
10 I've lived in the UK all my life. I've never lived _____. (6)
12 I've just _____ reading this novel – I've only read a few pages. (5)
14 I wear gloves to _____ my hands warm. (4)
17 You have to pay the fine – you have _____ choice. (2)
18 This quiz isn't difficult – it's the _____ I've ever done. (7)
21 'Do you want some pizza?' 'No thanks, I've already _____.' (5)
22 Usain Bolt _____ in his last World Championships in 2017. (8)
23 I'm really looking _____ to the party tonight. (7)
24 When someone _____ me money, I always pay it back. (5)
25 My phone was _____ than yours – it was £40 less. (7)
26 I don't want to cook – how _____ getting a takeaway? (5)
31 I'm so _____ I passed the test! (4)

SCORE 40

TOTAL 60

9 What a story!

- Past Perfect and Past Simple
- Conjunctions
- Feelings
- Homonyms
- Exclamations with *so* and *such*

Grammar   Past Perfect and Past Simple

1 Complete the story with the verb forms in the boxes.

| Past Simple | ~~lived~~ opened met appeared cut visited enjoyed lay killed looked |

| Past Perfect | ~~had died~~ had lost had stolen had tried had run had inherited |

Snow White and Rose Red

A long time ago there were two young girls who ¹ *lived* with their mother in a tiny cottage in the woods. Their father ² *had died* when they were young, and the family were now very poor. Snow White had blonde hair, and she was quiet and shy. She ³_____ helping her mother with the housework. Dark-haired Rose Red ⁴_____ her father's personality. She loved to be outside in the woods.

One cold, dark winter's night there was a knock at the door. Rose Red ⁵_____ it to find a bear outside. She was frightened, but the bear told her not to be afraid – he ⁶_____ his way in the wood and just needed to get warm. The girls let him in and the bear ⁷_____ down by the fire. Every night for the rest of the winter the bear ⁸_____ the family, and they grew to love him. Summer arrived, and the bear said he had to leave – a wicked dwarf ⁹_____ to steal his treasure the summer before, and he had to go and guard it.

A few days later, when the girls were walking in the forest, they ¹⁰_____ a dwarf whose beard was caught in a tree. The girls ¹¹_____ him free, but the dwarf just shouted at them for cutting his beautiful beard. They met the dwarf many times that summer, and he was always rude. Then one day when they saw him, he ¹²_____ terrified. He said he ¹³_____ miles to escape from a dangerous bear. Then, the girls' friendly bear ¹⁴_____ . The dwarf begged him to eat the girls not him, but the bear hit him with his big paw and ¹⁵_____ him. Suddenly, there was no bear, just a handsome prince. The prince explained how the dwarf ¹⁶_____ his treasure, and turned him into a bear. Now the dwarf was dead and the spell was broken.

Snow White married the prince and Rose Red married his brother, and they all lived happily ever after.

58   Unit 9 • What a story!

2 Put the verbs in brackets in the Past Perfect.
1. The girls _____ never _____ (see) a bear before.
2. The bear _____ already _____ (walk) a long way when he knocked on the cottage door.
3. The dwarf _____ never _____ (learn) good manners.
4. The bear _____ (follow) the dwarf through the forest.
5. The bear _____ (be) a prince the whole time!

3 Make sentences from the table.

A	B	C
1 I was hungry	because I'd / because I hadn't	crashed his car.
2 I was tired		spent it all on clothes.
3 I didn't have any money		eaten anything all day.
4 I was late for work		slept well the night before.
5 My mother was worried		set the alarm on my phone.
6 My father was angry		rung her for a week.

4 Complete the sentences using the verb once in the Past Simple and once in the Past Perfect.

had
1. I was hungry because I **hadn't had** any lunch.
2. I was really hungry this morning, so I **had** a huge breakfast.

go
3. I _____ to Rupert's party last night, it was great fun!
4. I didn't see Dawn at the party. She _____ home before I arrived.

give
5. My husband _____ me a lovely surprise for my birthday – dinner at The Ritz in London.
6. Julian was a poor man when he died. He _____ all his money to charity.

5 Look at the pictures. Complete the story using the Past Perfect.

1. Craig forgot to set his alarm and he woke up really late.
2. He missed the train to work, so he got a taxi.
3. The taxi broke down.
4. He arrived at work too late for his meeting.
5. His boss was very annoyed with him.
6. He felt ill in the afternoon, so he left work early.

Craig was sitting by the fire in his living room. He'd had a terrible day. **He'd forgotten to set his alarm the night before and …**
_____
_____
_____
_____

🔊 **9.1** Listen and check.

Unit 9 • What a story! 59

Conjunctions

6 Match a line in **A** with a line in **B**.

A	B
1 She didn't enjoy the dinner party because	☐ a I couldn't answer any of the questions.
2 Although he lived in Paris,	[1] b she didn't know anybody there.
3 He was thirsty, so	☐ c I was much older.
4 I didn't like tomatoes until	☐ d there was a train strike this morning.
5 I was so nervous in the exam that	☐ e he had a large glass of water.
6 She'd never been late for work before, but	☐ f he couldn't speak any French.

7 Join the pairs of sentences using the conjunction. Change one verb into the Past Perfect.

1 **when**
I read the text. I deleted it.
When I'd read the text, I deleted it.

2 **after**
I ate my dinner. I still felt hungry.

3 **although**
I didn't study for the exam. I got a good grade.

4 **before**
Tony told me how the story ended. I finished the book!

5 **until**
We didn't stop eating. We finished everything.

6 **as soon as**
I did my homework. I went to bed.

7 **so**
I was very rude to him. I rang and apologized.

8 **but**
I ran to the station. The train already left.

Things parents say

8 Here are some things parents say to their children. Complete the sentences with a conjunction.

| while (x2)   when   but   before   or   because   until |

1 *While* you were out with your friends, I was cleaning the house.

2 Don't fight with your sister _____ I'll send you to your room!

3 _____ someone says 'hello' to you, say 'hello' back.

4 You're laughing, _____ it's not funny.

5 Remember to brush your teeth _____ you go to bed.

6 You can't leave the table _____ everyone has finished their dinner.

7 Put your phone down _____ you're doing your homework.

8 You can't have any dessert _____ you didn't finish your vegetables.

🔊 **9.2** Listen and check.

A devoted dog

9 Read the text about **Dion** and **Gobi**. <u>Underline</u> the correct conjunctions.

One marathon man and his devoted dog

Many people around the world have read about Dion Leonard and his dog, Gobi. It is a heart-warming story about man's best friend – his dog! It all began when Dion, an ultra-marathon runner, was running in one of the world's most difficult challenges, the Gobi March – a series of seven marathons across the desert.

The run

The Gobi March is an annual 250-kilometre race across deserts around the world. Dion, a 42-year-old runner, had already run over a hundred kilometres across the Gobi Desert ¹*when / until* a stray dog decided to join him and ran with him for the rest of the day.

²*While / When* Dion woke up the next day, he found the dog outside his tent. She had slept there all night waiting for him. Dion tried his hardest to tell the dog to go away ³*although / because* he was worried that the small dog would get under the feet of all the runners. ⁴*However / So*, the dog refused to go, and crossed the finish line for that day's race with Dion. 'I started to speed off and I'm thinking, this dog won't last the whole day, but she was still with me at the end', said Dion. The loveable little dog slept with him in the tent that night. She had obviously been very lonely ⁵*because / before* she met Dion. Dion called his new friend Gobi and the pair stayed together ⁶*while / until* the end of the race.

The search

When the race was over, Dion left Gobi with a friend in China ⁷*while / until* he went home and arranged the necessary travel documents to bring her to the UK. Dion had been back in Scotland for a month ⁸*when / but* he heard that Gobi had gone missing, ⁹*after / so* he immediately flew back to China to search for her. ¹⁰*Before / After* searching for Gobi for five days, Dion had nearly given up all hope. He was very upset. ¹¹*Although / However* everyone was looking hard, no one could find Gobi.

Fortunately, a local person spotted Gobi ¹²*while / until* he was out walking. He had seen the posters and TV footage about Gobi and contacted Dion straight away. Gobi and Dion were both absolutely delighted to be reunited.

And now?

Dion brought Gobi back home to Edinburgh, Scotland. They now run together every day, and Gobi is helping Dion to train for his marathons. ¹³*While / Before* Dion met Gobi, training had always been rather lonely.

Dion has also written a book about their story, called *Finding Gobi*, and 20th Century Fox are thinking of making it into a movie.

---

10 Put the verbs in brackets into the Past Simple, Past Continuous or Past Perfect.

1 Dion _____ (*run*) in the Gobi March when he _____ (*meet*) Gobi.

2 Nobody knew where Gobi _____ (*live*) before he _____ (*start*) running with Dion.

3 Dion _____ (*not own*) a dog before Gobi.

4 Gobi _____ (*finish*) the Gobi March with Dion. She _____ (*manage*) to stay with him to the end of the race.

5 Dion _____ (*want*) to take Gobi back to Scotland.

6 He _____ nearly _____ (*complete*) the arrangements, when he _____ (*discover*) Gobi _____ (*go*) missing.

7 When he _____ (*return*) to China, people _____ still _____ (*look*) for Gobi.

8 A local man, who _____ (*go*) out walking one morning, _____ (*spot*) Gobi and _____ (*contact*) Dion.

9 He _____ (*know*) about the dog because he _____ (*see*) her story on TV.

10 Dion was delighted when he _____ (*hear*) the news about Gobi's discovery, because he _____ (*give*) up all hope of finding his small friend.

Unit 9 • What a story!

Vocabulary
Feelings

1 Read the clues and complete the crossword.

ACROSS

1 My teacher was _____ with me because I hadn't done my homework!
3 My daughter won the painting competition. I'm so _____ of her.
5 Sara doesn't have any close friends. She's very _____.
7 Richard has a lovely new girlfriend. I'm really _____.
8 My two-year-old daughter is really _____ of the dark.
9 Children usually feel _____ when their birthday is coming.

DOWN

2 I've got my driving test tomorrow. I'm so _____.
4 Walter was very _____ when his wife left him.
6 I've lived abroad for two years and I'm beginning to feel _____.

Homonyms

2 The words in the box have more than one meaning. Complete the pairs of lines with a word from the box.

| bear | spell | fan | match |

1 We saw a brown _____ in the mountains.

2 I can't _____ this weather.

3 This is a really exciting football _____.

4 I need a _____ to light the fire.

5 How do you _____ 'friend'?

6 The wicked witch made an evil _____.

7 I'm a big _____ of hip hop music.

8 It's so hot! Could you switch the _____ on?

3 Complete the pairs of lines with a word from the box.

| type | lie | fine | flat | fair |

1 a How many words a minute can you _____?
   b What _____ of dog do you have?
2 a 'How are you?' '_____, thanks. And you?'
   b I had to pay a £60 parking _____! I was so angry!
3 a He didn't tell me the truth. He told me a _____.
   b I'm tired. I'm going to _____ down for an hour.
4 a Everyone in my family is very _____. We all have blond hair and pale skin.
   b You gave her £10, but you only gave me £5. That's not _____!
5 a Do you live in a house or a _____?
   b Holland is a very _____ country.

62   Unit 9 • What a story!

Everyday English
Exclamations with *so* and *such*

Complete the conversations with *so*, *such*, *such a*, *so many* and *so much*.

1. **A** I was _____ surprised when I heard about Bella and Dan getting married!
   B Me too! It was _____ shock. I thought they hated each other!

2. **A** Look at this bedroom! Children you have made _____ mess!
   B Sorry! We were having _____ fun!

3. **A** There were _____ people at Sara's party!
   B I know! And there was _____ delicious food too! It was a great party!

4. **A** We had _____ terrible weather on holiday.
   B That's a shame. You really needed a bit of sunshine, you work _____ hard.

5. **A** Open your eyes, now!
   B Wow! This is _____ lovely surprise. I can't believe _____ of my friends are here for my birthday!
   A Well, it is your 30th!

🔊 9.3 Listen and check.

Go online for more skills and language practice.

REVIEW
Grammar

1. Put the verb in brackets in the Past Simple, Past Continuous or Past Perfect.

   1. When Darren and Martha _____ (*meet*) at the school reunion, they _____ (*not recognize*) each other because they _____ (*not see*) each other for 20 years.
   2. Jordan _____ already _____ (*cook*) dinner when Barbara _____ (*get*) home.
   3. While Yoko _____ (*have*) a shower, someone _____ (*ring*) the doorbell.
   4. Jenson _____ (*not do*) his homework, so the teacher _____ (*give*) him a detention.
   5. Keith _____ (*get*) home late from work, because he _____ (*miss*) the train.
   6. The children _____ (*scream*) often while they _____ (*watch*) the horror film.

2. Choose the correct conjunction.

   1. Bryan bought a Ferrari *when* / *however* / *although* he won £500,000 on the lottery.
   2. Please close the front door *when* / *while* / *until* you leave the house.
   3. I like to relax *as soon as* / *while* / *before* I'm on holiday.
   4. I rang Li *until* / *while* / *as soon as* I heard the news.
   5. I like Holly *when* / *because* / *so* she's so kind and generous.
   6. I'd planned to give a talk at the conference. *However,* / *Because* / *Although* I was sick and couldn't go.
   7. Can you feed the cat *until* / *before* / *while* I'm away?
   8. I woke up early *as soon as* / *although* / *however* I'd forgotten to set my alarm.
   9. Stop at a petrol station soon, *when* / *until* / *before* we run out of petrol!
   10. I'm going to study English *before* / *because* / *until* I can speak it perfectly.

Go online to Check your progress.

Unit 9 • What a story! 63

10 All-time greats

- Passives
- Active or passive?
- Past participles as adjectives
- Compound nouns
- Adverb + adjective
- On the phone

Grammar Passives

1 Complete the article about **Netflix** using the passive verb forms in the boxes.

NETFLIX – a streaming sensation

Netflix is a worldwide revolution. It has changed the way we watch TV. We don't even need a TV any longer to watch our favourite programmes – we can watch what we want, when we want, where we want on a TV, tablet, laptop, or phone!

The beginning

was refused   was offered   was founded   was fined

Netflix ¹_____ in 1997 after Reed Hastings, now the CEO, ²_____ $40 because he was late returning a copy of *Apollo 13* to a video rental shop. Netflix started as a DVD-by-mail rental business. In 2000, Netflix ³_____ to Blockbuster, another DVD rental company, but the offer ⁴_____. After better broadband made it possible for people to stream films to their TV, Netflix became the leader. It's now worth $60 billion and Blockbuster went bankrupt in 2010!

Netflix – the facts

| is watched   has been affected   are watched |
is estimated   was named   was awarded

The company's revenue ⁵_____ at $3.2 billion a year. It's available in 200 countries and the number is rising. In the US, Netflix ⁶_____ by more people than cable TV, and has nearly 55 million subscribers. Netflix has been streamed so heavily during prime time (nearly 37% of Internet traffic comes from Netflix) that video quality ⁷_____.

Netflix allows people to watch an entire series, called a 'box set', in one go. Box sets ⁸_____ by 60% of viewers. *Breaking Bad* is the most popular – so far 10.3 million people have watched the final series.

In 2014, Netflix ⁹_____ a Golden Globe, when Robin Wright ¹⁰_____ best actress in *House of Cards*.

What next?

| will be watched   will be made   will be developed |
is predicted

With classic series, like *The Crown* (a drama about Queen Elizabeth II), Netflix has become more and more popular. It ¹¹_____ that Netflix ¹²_____ in nearly every country around the world, and more and more of the programmes ¹³_____ by Netflix themselves. And even better streaming technology ¹⁴_____, so that heavy use will not affect picture quality.

2 Complete the questions. Choose the correct answer, **a** or **b**.

1 'Who ___ $40 for returning a late video?'
  'The CEO of Netflix.'
  a charged   **b** was charged

2 'Who ___ not to buy Netflix in 2000?'
  'Blockbuster.'
  a decided   **b** is decided

3 'What percentage of viewers ___ box sets?'
  '60%.'
  a watch   **b** are watched

4 'Who ___ a Golden Globe for best actress?'
  'Robin Wright.'
  a awarded   **b** was awarded

5 'What ___ to improve Netflix?'
  'Streaming technology.'
  a will develop   **b** will be developed

🔊 **10.1** Listen and check.

Forming the passive

3 Put the verb in brackets into the correct passive form.

Present Simple

1. 6% of the Earth's surface **is covered** (cover) by rainforest.
2. 40% of the Earth's oxygen _____ (produce) by rainforests.
3. We _____ (watch) by CCTV cameras everywhere we go.
4. What time _____ the post _____ (deliver)?
5. You _____ (cover) in dirt! What have you been doing?
6. A lot of information about our lives _____ (keep) on computers.

Past Simple

1. We **weren't affected** (not affect) by the flood, but our neighbours were.
2. _____ your car _____ (damage) in the accident?
3. The painting _____ (sell) for ten million dollars.
4. I _____ (introduce) to a very interesting man at the party.
5. The window _____ (break) during the robbery.
6. Where were you when these photos _____ (take)?

Present Perfect

1. All these issues **have been discussed** (discuss) many times before.
2. _____ you ever _____ (catch) speeding?
3. Have you heard? Catherine _____ (sack) from her job!
4. Oh no! Our plane _____ (delay) because of the snow.
5. Bill's doing really well at work. He _____ just _____ (promote) to area manager.

will

1. You**'ll be told** (tell) what to do when you arrive.
2. Your exam results _____ (email) to you.
3. Where _____ the next Olympic Games _____ (hold)?

Questions

4 Put the words in the correct order to make questions. Then choose the correct answer from the box.

> India   Russia   four   2018   over one billion
> ~~chickpeas, garlic and lemon juice~~

1 hummus / made / is / from / What / ?
A <u>What is hummus made from?</u>
B <u>Chickpeas, garlic and lemon juice.</u>

2 Hindi / spoken / Where / is / ?
A _____
B _____

3 every second / born / are / How many / babies / ?
A _____
B _____

4 held / Where / the World Cup / was / in 2018 / ?
A _____
B _____

5 were / When / Prince Harry / married / Meghan Markle / and / ?
A _____
B _____

6 have / seatbelts / How many / lives / been / by / 1975 / since / saved / ?
A _____
B _____

🔊 10.2 Listen and check.

Short answers

5 Correct the information in these sentences.
1. Paper is made from plastic.
   No, it isn't! It's made from wood.
2. Champagne is made in Scotland.
   _____
3. iPhones are made by Samsung.
   _____
4. The *Mona Lisa* was painted by Monet.
   _____
5. The Colosseum was built by the Greeks.
   _____

🔊 **10.3** Listen and check your answers.

The passive infinitive

6 Complete the sentences with the passive infinitive (*be* + past participle) of the verbs in the box.

| spend | ~~do~~ | serve | cancel | contact | knock down |
| clean | ban | take | | | |

1. The company is losing money. Something must **be done** to increase sales.
2. More money should _____ on education.
3. Please go and sit at the table. Dinner will _____ _____ in a few minutes.
4. Can you take my suit to the dry cleaner's? It needs to _____ before the wedding.
5. Smoking should _____ in all public places.
6. These pills must _____ with food twice a day.
7. The old factory is going to _____ tomorrow.
8. The football match had to _____ because of bad weather.
9. I'm not taking my phone, so I can't _____ _____ while I'm away.

Active or passive?

7 Choose the best way, **a** or **b**, to follow the sentences.
1. My parents live in a really old house.
   a Someone built it 200 years ago.
   b It was built 200 years ago.
2. Sue's living room looks beautiful. I love the colour!
   a It was decorated last month.
   b A man decorated it last month.
3. I bought a Fitbit, but I never wore it …
   a so I sold it on eBay.
   b so it was sold on eBay.
4. Do you like the chocolate cake?
   a It was made myself.
   b I made it myself.
5. The Crown Jewels are the most famous jewels in the world.
   a They can be seen at the Tower of London.
   b People can see them at the Tower of London.
6. We all have dinner together in the evening.
   a Then we usually watch TV.
   b Then the TV is usually watched.

Past participles as adjectives

8 Many past participles can be used as adjectives. Underline the correct adjective.
1. I hope I get the job. I'll be really *disappointed* / *amused* if I don't.
2. She was *heartbroken* / *determined* when her boyfriend left her for another woman.
3. We were *amused* / *shocked* to hear that Nick's in hospital. What's the matter with him?
4. Ruben worked really hard. He was *annoyed* / *determined* to do well in his exams.
5. I really wanted to go to Elaine's New Year's Eve party so I was *horrified* / *delighted* when I got an invitation.
6. My dad was *horrified* / *amused* when he saw my latest tattoo. He hates tattoos!
7. My new laptop isn't working properly. I'm really *annoyed* / *delighted*.
8. I was *surprised* / *determined* to see Erika at work this morning. I thought she was sick.
9. Their daughter is so *disappointed* / *talented*. She can play the cello, piano, and violin really well.
10. I didn't laugh out loud at the play, but I was *talented* / *amused*.

Unit 10 • All-time greats

The history of paper

9 Read the text. Put the verbs in brackets in the correct tense, active or passive.

The history of paper

Today, paper ¹_____ (use) for hundreds of everyday things – books and newspapers, of course, but also money, stamps, cups, bags, and even some clothes.

Long ago, before paper ²_____ (invent), people ³_____ (write) on animal skins, bones, and stones. Then in 2700 BC, the Egyptians ⁴_____ (start) to make papyrus, which was similar to paper. But the first real paper ⁵_____ (invent) in AD 105 by a Chinese government official, Ts'ai Lun. It ⁶_____ (make) from a mixture of plants and cloth. The Chinese ⁷_____ (keep) their invention secret for centuries.

Finally, in the 10th century, paper ⁸_____ (bring) to Europe by the Arabs. The first European paper mill ⁹_____ (build) in Spain in 1150. Since the 18th century, most paper ¹⁰_____ (make) out of wood, because it's much stronger than cloth.

Paper today

In the US, Japan, and Europe an average person ¹¹_____ (use) between 250 and 300 kilos of paper every year. In the US, one billion dollars worth of trees are thrown away every year! However, the good news is that paper can ¹²_____ (recycle). Paper recycling worldwide ¹³_____ (expect) to grow from 43% to 61%. Today we have many alternatives to using paper. Nearly all communication ¹⁴_____ (do) electronically, and books, magazines, and newspapers can all ¹⁵_____ (read) on electronic devices.

10 Match the question words and answers.

1 When? (x2)	☐ a Ts'ai Lun.
2 Where? (x2)	☐ b About 300 kg.
3 Who/by?	☐ c In Spain.
4 How long?	☐ d In AD 105.
5 How much?	☐ e Since the 18th century.
	☐ f In China.
	☐ g In the 10th century.

11 Write the questions using the passive.

1 'When _was_ paper _invented_?'
   'In AD 105.'
2 'Where _____ paper first _____?'
   'In China.'
3 'Who _____ the first real paper _____ by?'
   'Ts'ai Lun.'
4 'When _____ paper _____ to Europe?'
   'In the 10th century.'
5 'Where _____ the first European paper mill _____?'
   'In Spain.'
6 'How long _____ paper _____ from wood?'
   'Since the 18th century.'
7 'How much paper _____ by each person every year?'
   'About 300 kg.'

🔊 **10.4** Listen and check.

12 Correct the sentences.

1 Before paper, shells were used to write on.
   No, they weren't! Animal skins were used.
2 The first real paper was invented by a Japanese government official.
   _____
3 Paper was brought to Europe by the Spanish.
   _____
4 Paper has been made out of wood for 100 years.
   _____
5 Paper recycling is expected to decline worldwide.
   _____

🔊 **10.5** Listen and check.

Vocabulary
Compound nouns

1 Write a word to make three compound nouns.

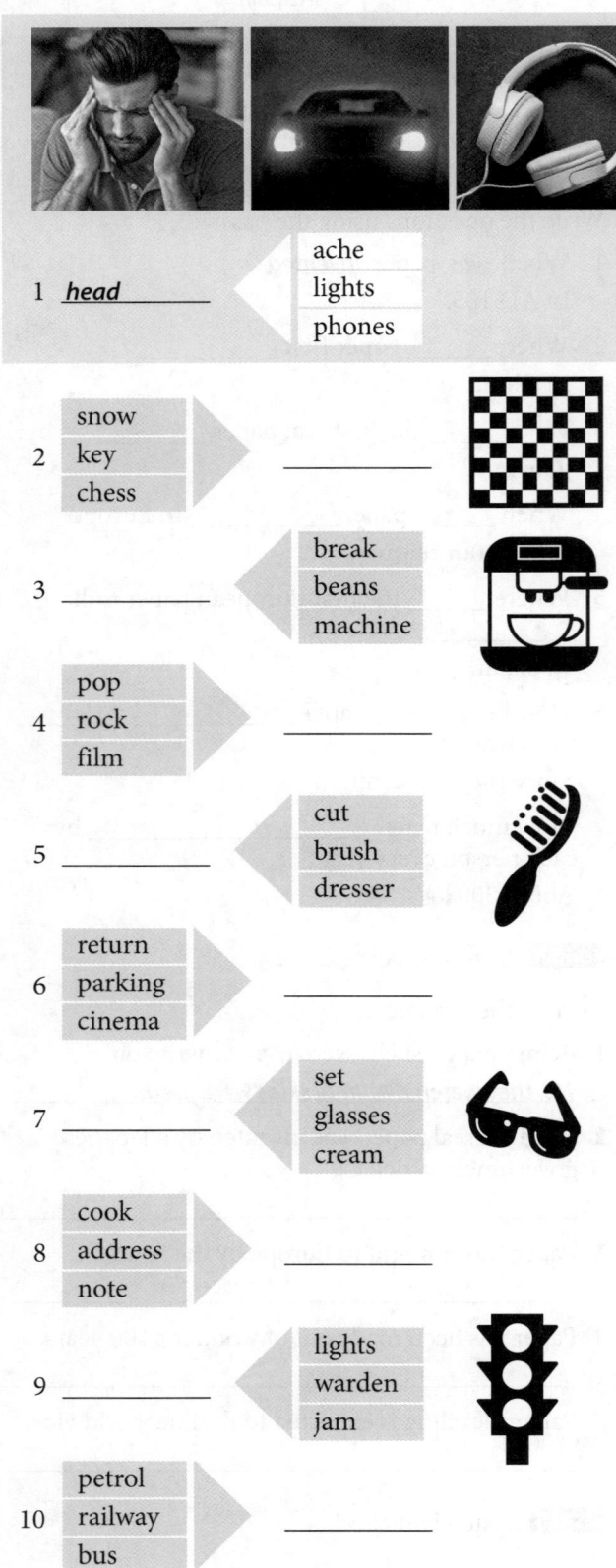

1 _head_ — ache / lights / phones

2 snow / key / chess — _____

3 _____ — break / beans / machine

4 pop / rock / film — _____

5 _____ — cut / brush / dresser

6 return / parking / cinema — _____

7 _____ — set / glasses / cream

8 cook / address / note — _____

9 _____ — lights / warden / jam

10 petrol / railway / bus — _____

2 Answer the questions using a compound noun.

1 What do people take an aspirin for? _A headache._
2 Where do you look for recipes? _____
3 What do you type on? _____
4 If you park in the wrong place, what might you get? _____
5 What should you put on your skin before you sunbathe? _____
6 What is beautiful to watch at the end of the day? _____
7 What must you switch on when you're driving at night? _____
8 What do you buy to travel somewhere and come back? _____

Adverb + adjective

3 Complete the sentences with an adverb in **A** and an adjective in **B**.

A	B
well	written
	equipped
	done
	paid
badly	known
	behaved
	dressed

1 Paula's job isn't very _____. She's 32, and still has to live at home.
2 My children are really _____. I can't take them anywhere!
3 Your kitchen is really _____. It looks like a restaurant kitchen!
4 Would you like your steak rare, medium, or _____?
5 Victoria Beckham is always _____. You never see her in jeans and a T-shirt!
6 This novel is so _____! I could write a better one myself!
7 I feel _____ today. I chose my clothes in a rush.
8 Zac Efron is a very _____ Hollywood actor. I've seen most of his films.

Everyday English
On the phone

Complete the conversations with the words from the boxes.

1 | missed call   get back   speak   back   calling   left |

A Hi Andrew. Did you listen to the voicemail I ¹_____ you?
B No, sorry. I saw a ²_____ from you, but completely forgot to ring you ³_____.
A No worries. Listen. I'm ⁴_____ because I can't make this Saturday. My brother's on his own with the kids, and I said I'd help him. Would you like to come round? It'll be great fun!
B Umm, I'm not sure … Can I ⁵_____ to you on that later?
A Sure. ⁶_____ to you later, then.

2 | get in touch   replies   breaking up   signal
    got back   hear   send |

A Hi, Lara. Sorry to disturb you. I'm on my way to work … and … trying …
B Sorry, I couldn't ¹_____ that. You're ²_____.
A Sorry, the ³_____ is terrible here, lots of tall buildings … Anyway, I'm calling because I need to ⁴_____ with Olivia. I've emailed her, but she hasn't ⁵_____ to me.
B Have you tried her mobile? She always ⁶_____ to texts.
A Well, I thought I had her number, but I don't.
B Don't worry. I'll ⁷_____ it to you.

3 | could   through   call   line   how   hold |

A Good morning. Reception. ¹_____ can I help you?
B Hello. ²_____ I speak to Rebecca Jenkins, please?
A Just a moment. I'll put you ³_____ to her secretary … I'm afraid the ⁴_____'s busy. Would you like to ⁵_____?
B No, thanks. I'll ⁶_____ back later.

🔊 10.6 Listen and check.

▶ Go online for more skills and language practice.

REVIEW

Read about the app developer, **Robert Nay**. Put the verbs in brackets into the correct tense, active or passive.

Robert Nay
Inventor of Bubble Ball,
a multi-level physics puzzle app

Robert Nay was only 14 years old when he ¹_____ (develop) Bubble Ball, a 72-level physics puzzle game. In the first two weeks of its release it ²_____ (download) two million times from Apple iTunes. Not bad, when the average mobile game only receives a few hundred downloads. Bubble Ball ³_____ (overtake) the hugely successful *Angry Birds*, and ⁴_____ (become) the number one free app game. Nay wanted to develop an app that could ⁵_____ (use) by children of all abilities.

The puzzles ⁶_____ (range) from simple to very challenging. At each level you ⁷_____ (give) tools to help you complete the level.

'My friend's dad ⁸_____ (suggest) I try to make an iPhone app, and I thought it would be really cool and ⁹_____ (decide) to give it a try … I came up with the idea for the game by myself, but it ¹⁰_____ (influence) by other games I liked,' said Nay.

Bubble Ball ¹¹_____ now _____ (download) over 16 million times and Nay now has his own game development company. His advice to young people is: 'You can do amazing things if you just try.'

▶ Go online to Check your progress.

11 People with a passion

- Present Perfect Continuous
- Present Perfect Simple and Continuous
- Tense review
- Stages of life
- Finding the right words

Grammar
Present Perfect Simple and Continuous

1 Match a line in **A** with a line in **B**.

A	B
1 I've been doing my homework I've done my homework,	for three hours. I'm exhausted. so I can go out with my friends now.
2 My son's been collecting football cards He's collected	nearly two hundred already. since he was six.
3 Ria has been learning English She's learned three languages	in three years! She's amazing. for just six months and she's fluent.

2 Complete the email from Penny to her friend Katie with a phrase from the boxes.

Present Perfect Simple

| has applied   has she started   hasn't succeeded |
| have attached   ~~haven't heard~~ |

Present Perfect Continuous

| have been working   has been trying   has been collecting |
| have you been doing   has been looking for |

From: pen.mulligan4@yahboo.com   To: kat_tak@hotspot.co.uk
Subject: It's been ages!

Hi Katie,

How are you? I ¹ *haven't heard* from you for ages. I'd love to get your news – what ² _____ ?

How are the kids? What about Nancy? ³ _____ school yet? Does she like it? And Max? Is he still crazy about football? My Freddy is too, but he isn't as good as Max – he ⁴ _____ to get into the school football team, but he ⁵ _____ yet.

Rob ⁶ _____ a new job. You know how much he hates working for City Trading Ltd. He ⁷ _____ to over ten companies, and has finally got two interviews next week. Fingers crossed!

How's your work? Are you still enjoying teaching as much as ever? I expect you ⁸ _____ too hard as usual! My work's still boring, but at least I got a pay rise last year.

Email me soon. It would be lovely to hear from you. Even better, come and visit us, we'd love to see you and the family. It's been too long!

Love,

Penny xx

PS I ⁹ _____ a photo of football-mad Freddy with his card collection! He ¹⁰ _____ them for just a few months and he's already got 50!

70 Unit 11 • People with a passion

Present Perfect Continuous

3 Match a line in **A** with a line in **B**.

A	B
1 Max's been playing football in the rain.	a It's all over the floor.
2 Katie's been checking her email.	b His hair is covered with paint.
3 Grandpa's been digging in the garden.	c There are a lot to reply to.
4 Sue and Ken have been cooking for friends.	d His boots and shorts are muddy.
5 The kids have been washing the dog.	e Everything's so clean and tidy.
6 The baby's been throwing his food.	f His back hurts.
7 Grandma's been doing the housework.	g The house smells of onion and garlic.
8 Dad's been decorating the bedroom.	h There's soap and water everywhere.

4 Complete the sentences with the verbs in the box in the Present Perfect Continuous.

cry   try   save   sunbathe   study   wait

1 Why are you so late? I _____ for over an hour!
2 I _____ to speak to my sister for days, but she's not answering her phone.
3 Bonnie _____ medicine for five years, and there are still three more years to go.
4 Dave and Julie _____ really hard to get a deposit to buy a house.
5 Look at Cooper's red face! I think he _____.
6 What's the matter with little Nina? She _____ for the last five minutes.

Making questions

5 Complete the questions with the verbs in the Present Perfect Continuous.

1 How long _____ you _____ (*learn*) English? You're very good!
2 The streets are wet. _____ it _____ ? (*rain*)
3 I didn't know Andy could speak Chinese. How long _____ he _____ it? (*learn*)
4 _____ you _____ (*watch*) that new detective series on Netflix? It's brilliant!
5 How long _____ Cody _____ (*go out*) with Viviana?
6 What _____ the children _____ (*do*)? They're filthy!

Present Perfect Simple or Continuous?

6 Choose the correct form of the verb.

1 'Hi Lily! How are you?'
   'Hi! Fine thanks. Good to see you. What ___ for the last few months?'
   a have you been doing
   b have you done

2 'What was that crash?'
   'It was Bo. He ___ a window playing football!'
   a 's broken
   b 's been breaking

3 'Hanna and Dominic are a lovely couple'.
   'Yes, they are. They ___ together since university.'
   a 've gone out
   b 've been going out

4 'Do you want anything to eat?'
   'No, thanks. I ___ a sandwich.'
   a 've had
   b 've been having

5 'Why are you all wet?'
   'Because it ___.'
   a 's rained
   b 's been raining

6 'Have you thanked Aunt Matilda for the present?'
   'Yes, I ___ her a card.'
   a 've sent
   b 've been sending

7 'How long ___ the guitar? He's really good!'
   'Not long, but he practises every day.'
   a has Greg played
   b has Greg been playing

8 'Ouch!' I ___ my head!'
   'Are you OK?'
   a 've bumped
   b 've been bumping

9 'Is this your phone?'
   'Oh, yes! Thank you! I ___ it for ages.'
   a 've looked
   b 've been looking for

10 'Oh dear! That is a bad cold. How long ___ it?'
   'For ages.'
   a have you had
   b have you been having

🔊 **11.1** Listen and check.

Unit 11 • People with a passion   71

Present Perfect Simple or Continuous?

7 Put the verbs in brackets into the Present Perfect Simple or the Present Perfect Continuous.

1. I'm hot because I _____ (run).
2. Ouch! I _____ (cut) my finger!
3. _____ you _____ (hear) Ed Sheeran's latest song?
4. She's tired because she _____ (shop) all day.
5. Sorry! I _____ (break) one of your glasses.
6. I _____ (read) this book for six months now.
7. Drew _____ (paint) the bedroom, but he hasn't finished yet.
8. Look what Grandma _____ (give) me for my birthday! A bike!
9. I _____ (lose) my wallet! Where did I put it?
10. There's my wallet. I _____ (look) for it for ages.

8 Correct the mistakes in these sentences.

1. How long you have been studying English?
2. She's living in Japan for two years now.
3. Have you been knowing Robin for a long time?
4. She been working very hard lately.
5. What have you to eat today?
6. George hasn't been finishing his homework yet.
7. The plane hasn't been arrived yet.
8. I've always been wanting to see the Northern Lights.
9. Steve has been going to the shops. He'll be back soon.
10. It's raining for ages. When will it stop? I want to go for a walk.
11. What have your children done? They're filthy!
12. I've been having a dog for five years now. I can't imagine life without her.

Tense review

9 Complete the conversation with the correct tense, Present or Past Simple, Present Perfect Simple or Continuous.

Alex Hi Rob! I ¹_____ (see) you for ages! How are you?

Rob Hi, Alex. I'm fine, thanks – really good. And you?

Alex I'm OK, thanks. What ²_____ you _____ (do) since I last ³_____ (see) you?

Rob Not a lot. I ⁴_____ (start) a new job last month. It's still in advertising, but with a new company.

Alex How long ⁵_____ you _____ (work) in advertising?

Rob For five years. I really ⁶_____ (enjoy) it ... most of the time. Anyway, what about you? What's new?

Alex Well, Diana and I are finally going to get married.

Rob That's fantastic! Congratulations! How long ⁷_____ you two _____ (go out) together?

Alex It's eight years now. We ⁸_____ (meet) at your wedding – don't you remember?

Rob Of course I ⁹_____ (remember). How could I forget?! That's great news. I can't wait to tell Penny. She'll be delighted.

🔊 **11.2** Listen and check.

An unusual collectible

10 Look at the photos and *quickly* read the text.
  1 Who are the celebrities?
  2 Why are they important to Paul Fraser?

11 Read the text again and complete it with the verbs in the correct tense.

Paul Fraser
Celebrity hair collector!

Celebrity culture ¹ *has arrived* (*arrive*)! We ² _____ never _____ (*be*) more interested in the latest celebrity news and gossip. And some fans ³ _____ just _____ (*not want*) to read about their favourite celebrity, they want more – an autograph, a selfie or even a lock of their hair! So, believe it or not, there are professional hair collectors who ⁴ _____ (*make*) money by selling the locks of celebrities!

Paul Fraser is a UK professional collector of all kinds of things, including … hair! He ⁵ _____ (*collect*) the hair of famous people for some years. He ⁶ _____ (*be*) a collector of stamps, coins, fine art, and antiques for a long time, but a few years ago, Paul ⁷ _____ (*realize*) that the best way to make money was to invest in things that are one of a kind, such as a lock of a celebrity's hair. In 2016, a US auction house in Texas ⁸ _____ (*sell*) a lock of John Lennon's hair for an amazing $35,000.

Paul Fraser now ⁹ _____ (*own*) a lock of Paul McCartney's hair, and he also ¹⁰ _____ (*have*) Michael Jackson's, Marilyn Monroe's, Napoleon's, John Kennedy's, and even Charles Dickens's hair in his collection. When the celebrity is dead, the hair is worth more! However, in 2011 someone ¹¹ _____ (*buy*) a lock of Justin Bieber's hair on eBay for $40,668!

Paul charges $570 for just one strand of hair! He ¹² _____ (*sell*) hair for the last few years on his website, Paul Fraser Collectibles, alongside his other collections.

So – what's the highest amount of money someone ¹³ _____ ever _____ (*pay*) for a lock of celebrity hair? And whose head ¹⁴ _____ it _____ (*belong*) to? It was Elvis Presley's, and it ¹⁵ _____ (*cost*) $115,000!

Historian, Leo Braudy, says, 'to own a genuine* artefact* from a widely recognised cultural figure – even if it's hair – is highly attractive.'

This certainly seems to be true!

genuine real
artefact an object of historical or cultural interest

Celebrity hair for sale
BID NOW
Auction ends in 2 days
$800
BUY IT NOW
○ Add to basket
○ Add to wishlist

Justin Beiber
Elvis Presley
Marilyn Monroe

12 Complete the questions using the verbs in brackets. Then answer them.

  1 What *does* Paul Fraser *do* (*do*)?
    He's a professional collector.
  2 What kind of things _____ he _____ (*collect*)?
  3 How long _____ he _____ (*collect*) celebrity hair?
  4 Why _____ he _____ (*start*) collecting hair?
  5 How much _____ John Lennon's hair _____ (*sell*) for?
  6 _____ Paul _____ (*own*) Lennon's hair?
  7 How much _____ Paul Fraser _____ (*charge*) for a strand of hair?
  8 What's the greatest amount someone _____ ever _____ (*pay*) for a lock of hair? Whose hair _____ (*be*) it?

🔊 **11.3** Listen and check.

Unit 11 • People with a passion   73

Vocabulary
Stages of life

1 Put the words into the correct column in the table. Some may go into more than one column.

> wedding   pregnant   widow   dead   funeral
> midwife   widower   get divorced   cemetery
> give birth   due   gravestone   die of
> get engaged   honeymoon   expecting
> pass away   Congratulations!

Birth	Marriage	Death

2 Match the lines in A to the lines in B.

A

1. Cora and Sebastian are so in love.
2. My grandfather passed away last week.
3. Ella is expecting a baby.
4. Tina's been a widow for a long time.
5. The wedding was last weekend.
6. Lisa and Alan got engaged!
7. Dora gave birth to a beautiful baby girl.
8. Eric and Petra got divorced three years ago.

B

- [ ] a They're on honeymoon in Barbados now.
- [ ] b Her husband died over ten years ago.
- [ ] c The funeral is next Friday.
- [ ] d He's still single, but she remarried last year.
- [ ] e He proposed on Valentine's Day.
- [1] f They're getting married in the spring.
- [ ] g She's due on May 10.
- [ ] h She was over four kilos!

Everyday English
Finding the right words

Complete the dialogue with the lines in the box.

> a I'm so sorry. He was such a kind man.
> b Was it a boy or girl? How much did it weigh?
> c Oh dear! I hope he feels better soon.
> d Wow! They're going to be busy! Give them my congratulations.
> e What a shame! They seemed such a happy couple.
> f Congratulations! It's about time. You've been going out for three years!

1
A Have you heard the news? Jill and Simon are getting divorced.
B _____

2
A Harry's been in bed with the flu for a week!
B _____

3
A Maggie had the baby at six in the morning!
B _____

4
A We're getting married next spring!
B _____

5
A My grandad passed away last week.
B _____

6
A Karen and Tim are expecting twins!
B _____

🔊 **11.4** Listen and check.

Go online for more skills and language practice.

REVIEW

Read the interview with the actress, **Juliette Binoche** (JB). Put the verbs in brackets into the correct tense:

- Present Simple
- Present Continuous
- Past Simple
- Past Continuous
- Present Perfect Simple
- Present Perfect Continuous

The 60-second interview

Juliette Binoche was born in Paris. She is an actress and also a passionate painter. She is involved in politics and fundraising for charities. She has two children, a boy and a girl.

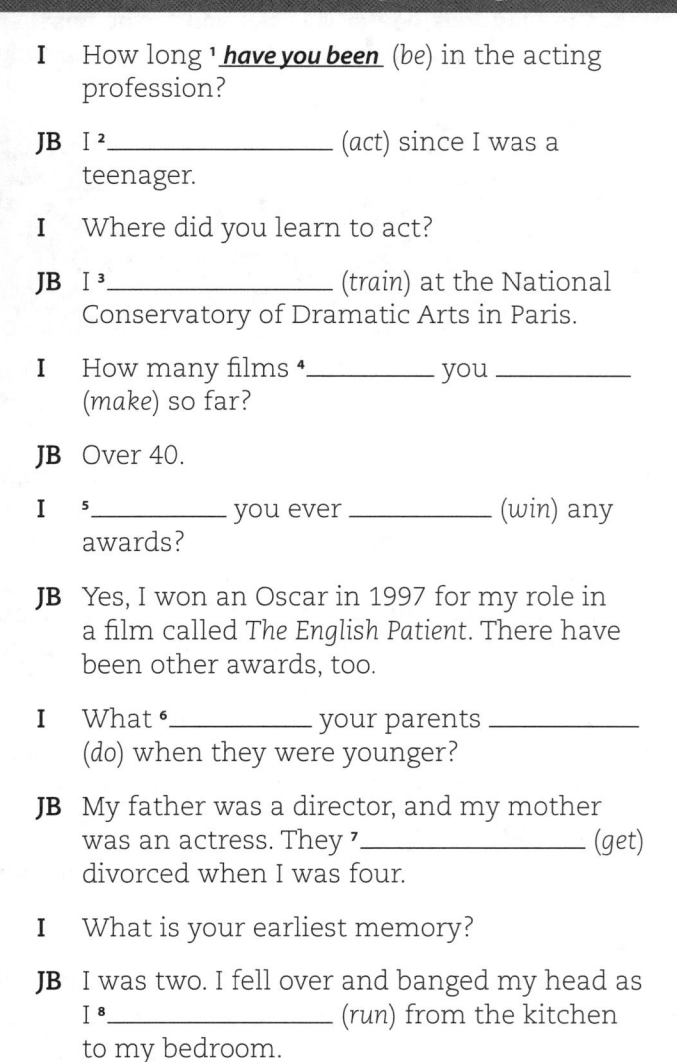

I   How long **¹ _have you been_** (be) in the acting profession?

JB I ² _____ (act) since I was a teenager.

I   Where did you learn to act?

JB I ³ _____ (train) at the National Conservatory of Dramatic Arts in Paris.

I   How many films ⁴ _____ you _____ (make) so far?

JB Over 40.

I   ⁵ _____ you ever _____ (win) any awards?

JB Yes, I won an Oscar in 1997 for my role in a film called *The English Patient*. There have been other awards, too.

I   What ⁶ _____ your parents _____ (do) when they were younger?

JB My father was a director, and my mother was an actress. They ⁷ _____ (get) divorced when I was four.

I   What is your earliest memory?

JB I was two. I fell over and banged my head as I ⁸ _____ (run) from the kitchen to my bedroom.

I   What ⁹ _____ you _____ (do) in your free time?

JB I adore gardening.

I   What are you doing now?

JB I ¹⁰ _____ (shoot) a film set in Ireland. It's a political thriller.

I   What's the best book you ¹¹ _____ ever _____ (read)?

JB *Talking with Angels* by Gitta Mallasz.

I   ¹² _____ you _____ (prefer) cats or dogs?

JB I love them both.

I   When ¹³ _____ you last _____ (cry)?

JB Today, while I ¹⁴ _____ (rehearse). It's my job to bring emotions to life.

I   What is your greatest achievement?

JB The film *Three Colours Blue* is one of the best films I ¹⁵ _____ ever _____ (make).

I   What is your motto on life?

JB Don't look back. Live in the present.

➤ **Go online** to Check your progress.

Unit 11 • People with a passion

12 You never know …

- First Conditional
- Second Conditional
- Conjunctions
- *bring* and *take*, *come* and *go*
- Prepositions
- Thank you and goodbye!

Grammar
First Conditional

1 Look at the travel website. Complete the text with the phrases in the box.

> 'll enjoy   book   'll include   'll want to do   are
> 'll have   bring   feel   won't be disappointed
> 're looking for   'll love   like   'll give   aren't

2 Your friend is planning to go on the diving holiday. Write questions about possible problems.

1 What / do / not get / the time off work?
   What will you do if you don't get the time off work?

2 What / do / feel scared?
   _____

3 What / do / not like / the other people on the trip?
   _____

4 What / do / get seasick?
   _____

5 What do / fail / scuba diving course?
   _____

6 What / do / not see a great white shark?
   _____

3 Match the answers with the questions in 2.
   a ☐ I'll take a pill and lie down.
   b [1] I'll take unpaid holiday.
   c ☐ I'll ask for my money back.
   d ☐ I'll take it again.
   e ☐ I'll be fine spending time by myself.
   f ☐ I'll take some deep breaths, and try and relax.

🔊 12.1 Listen and check.

Divers Deep Sea Discovery

The experience of a lifetime!

Do you like adventure and pushing yourself to the limit? If your answer is yes, you ¹ *'ll enjoy* this unusual 5-night break. Our luxurious boats will take you to the best locations to see the most magnificent ocean creatures.

✱ If you ² _____ an unforgettable experience, you ³ _____ ! This deep water site is full of incredible marine life.

✱ If you ⁴ _____ passionate about sea life, you ⁵ _____ seeing sharks, dolphins, and whales in their natural environment.

✱ If you ⁶ _____ brave enough, you ⁷ _____ the opportunity to get close to one of the world's most powerful predators, the great white shark, in complete safety.

✱ If you ⁸ _____ learning new skills, you ⁹ _____ our one-day scuba diving course. You'll receive a certificate at the end of the course.

Our best deal ever!

✱ If you ¹⁰ _____ a friend, we'll give you both a 10% discount.

✱ If you ¹¹ _____ before the end of the month, we ¹² _____ free underwater photos of your dive.

✱ If you ¹³ _____ completely satisfied with your trip, we ¹⁴ _____ you your money back.

Don't miss out on the adventure of a lifetime! What are you waiting for? Book now!

76 Unit 12 • You never know …

Second Conditional

Dreams

4 Paula works at a department store in London. Read about her real life, then complete the sentences about her dreams.

Paula's real life

She lives in a tiny apartment.
She gets up at 6.30 a.m.
She works ten hours a day.
She never goes on holiday.
She wears cheap jeans and T-shirts.

If I were rich, …

1 I _'d live_ _____ in a cottage with a garden.
2 I _____ until 9.00 a.m.
3 I _____ long hours – just four hours a day.
4 I _____ on holiday to Thailand.
5 I _____ designer clothes.

5 Write the questions about Paula's dreams.

If you were rich, …

1 '_Where would you live_ _____?'
   'In a cottage.'
2 '_____?'
   'At 9.00 a.m.'
3 '_____?'
   'Four hours a day.'
4 '_____?'
   'To Thailand.'
5 '_____?'
   'Designer clothes.'

If only I lived in the country …

6 Read the facts about Paula and look at the photos. Complete the sentences.

Fact 1 Paula lives in a small flat in London.

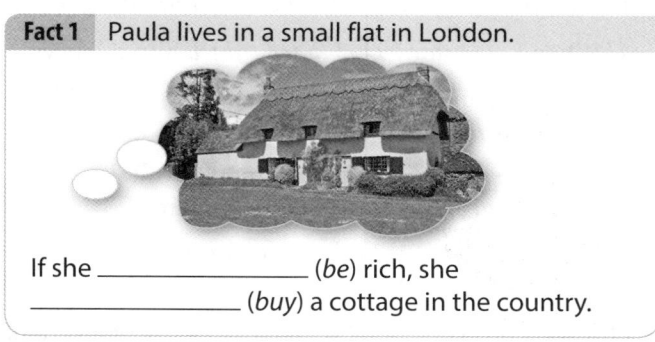

If she _____ (*be*) rich, she _____ (*buy*) a cottage in the country.

Fact 2 She can't have pets in her flat.

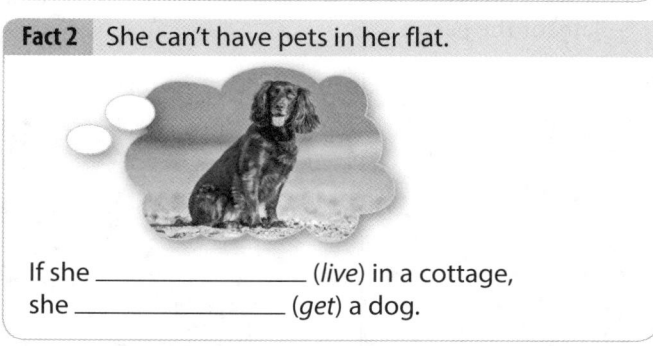

If she _____ (*live*) in a cottage, she _____ (*get*) a dog.

Fact 3 She doesn't have a garden.

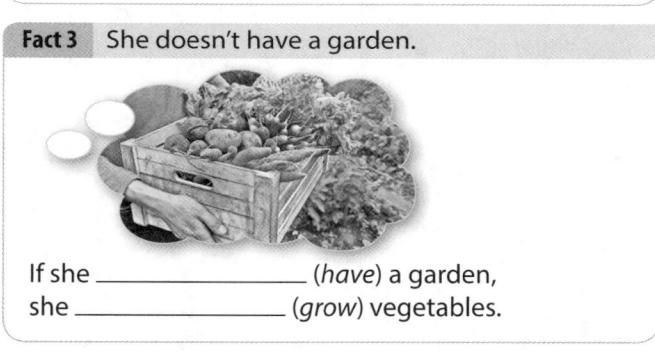

If she _____ (*have*) a garden, she _____ (*grow*) vegetables.

Fact 4 She can't drive.

If she _____ (*get*) her driving licence, she _____ (*drive*) a Land Rover.

Fact 5 She doesn't have any free time.

If she _____ (*have*) more free time, she _____ (*take up*) painting.

Unit 12 • You never know …

First or Second Conditional?

7 Underline the correct form of the verb in *italics*.

1 If I *am / were* younger, I *'ll travel / 'd travel* the world.
2 When I *see / saw* Jack, I *'ll tell / 'd tell* him the news.
3 Are you going shopping? I *'ll come / 'd come* with you if you *like / liked*.
4 If you *come / came* from my country, you *'ll understand / 'd understand* the problem.
5 If my house *is / was* as big as yours, I *'ll get / 'd get* a cleaner.
6 If you *don't get / didn't get* ready soon, we *'ll be / 'd be* late for the party.

8 Put the verbs in brackets into the correct form.

1 What _____ you _____ (*do*) if you _____ (*win*) the lottery?
2 If I _____ (*be*) taller, I _____ (*join*) the police force.
3 We _____ (*not go out*) this afternoon if the weather _____ (*be*) bad.
4 If I _____ (*not have*) a job, I _____ (*get up*) at ten o'clock every day.
5 If you _____ (*not study*) hard, you _____ (*not get*) into university.
6 I _____ (*buy*) those shoes if they _____ (*not cost*) so much.
7 Don't worry – if your boss _____ (*call*), I _____ (*tell*) him you're not feeling well.
8 If I _____ (*speak*) perfect English, I _____ (*not have to study*) at all!

might

9 Rewrite the sentences using *might*.

1 Perhaps it'll rain tomorrow.
   It might rain tomorrow.
2 Perhaps we'll go to Spain on holiday.
   _____
3 Perhaps I'll go to the cinema tonight.
   _____
4 Perhaps we'll go out for dinner on Saturday.
   _____
5 Perhaps I'll get a bike for my birthday.
   _____

10 Underline the correct form of the verb in *italics*.

1 Don't wait for me. I *'ll be / might be* late. It depends on when I finish work.
2 'What are you doing tonight?'
   'I don't know. I *'m going out / might go out*, or I *might stay in / 'm staying in*.'
3 'Bye! I *'ll see / might see* you this evening!'
   'See you later! Dinner will be ready at 7.00.'
4 'What are you cooking tonight?'
   'I haven't decided yet. I *'m going to make / might make* a chicken curry.'
5 I *might take / 'm taking* Jenny to Paris for our wedding anniversary. I booked it yesterday.
6 Cathy and Stefan *are going to get / might get* married! They got engaged last week.

Conjunctions

11 Complete the sentences with *if* or *when*.

1 We'll stay at home _____ the weather's bad.
2 I'll give you a ring _____ I get home.
3 _____ you gave up smoking, you'd be much healthier.
4 I'll do the washing up _____ the film ends.
5 _____ you don't work hard, you won't pass your exams.
6 We don't mind camping, but _____ we had more money, we'd stay in expensive hotels.
7 I'm not very hungry now, but I might have a sandwich _____ the plane takes off.
8 What would you do _____ you found £1,000 on the street?

Supervolcano

12 Read the introduction about supervolcanoes.

1 What are they?
2 How many are there?
3 When did the last one erupt?

Supervolcano!

If a supervolcano erupted, ¹ *the whole world would freeze* !

A supervolcano is an extremely large and powerful volcano that can change the world's climate and its ecosystems. It's 1,000 times more powerful than an ordinary volcano. There are about 40 supervolcanoes on earth, but, fortunately, they don't erupt often – the last one erupted in Indonesia 74,000 years ago.

Yellowstone National Park – Wyoming, US

Unbelievably, one of the world's top tourist attractions, Yellowstone National Park, is a supervolcano. If you go there, ² _____ ! However, you don't need to worry – the last time it erupted was 640,000 years ago.

What would happen if the Yellowstone volcano erupted today?

Day 1 – Yellowstone Park, US
³ _____ , huge amounts of hot ash and rock would shoot up into the air at 250 kph. The cities of Denver and Salt Lake would be destroyed immediately, and ⁴ _____ . Eventually, the ash would cover ¾ of the US; there would be no drinking water or crops.

Week 1 – Europe
The whole of Europe would be covered in a grey cloud. Summer would turn to winter and in some places ⁵ _____ . No European country would be able to grow food for five years.

The next three months – worldwide
90% of our sunlight would be lost and the world would experience a volcanic winter. The tropical forests would die, and food crops in warm countries, such as India and China, would fail. Only countries near the North and South Poles could survive. Iceland would do well because a lot of its food is grown in greenhouses so ⁶ _____ .

Eventually
Mankind could become as extinct as the dinosaurs!

Should we be worried?

Fortunately, scientists say that the supervolcano will not erupt in the near future. They think such events are unlikely to happen for the next few centuries.

However, there are many volcanoes around the world that could erupt at any time, and if they do, ⁷ _____ ! One of the volcanoes that scientists are watching is Ol Doinyo Lengai in Tanzania. ⁸ _____ , it will destroy local villages, and possibly even a 19,000-year-old historic site.

The good news is that volcanoes and supervolcanoes are well-monitored by experts, so we can all get on with our lives and stop worrying.

13 Read the article and write the phrases in the correct place in the text.

a … you'll walk on a 9,000m² volcano
b … it might be able to send some food to the rest of the world
c … the sea would freeze
d ~~… the whole world would freeze~~
e … they will cause great damage
f If the volcano erupted …
g If it erupts …
h … 87,000 people would die

14 Read the article again. Complete the sentences.

If the Yellowstone supervolcano erupted, …

1 … Denver and Salt Lake City _____ destroyed.
2 … the US _____ no drinking water.
3 … summer _____ to winter in Europe.
4 … European countries _____ grow food.
5 … the tropical forests worldwide _____ .
6 … countries near the Equator _____ survive.
7 … only Iceland _____ well.

If Ol Doinyo Lengai erupts, …

8 … it _____ great damage.
9 … people _____ their homes.
10 … a very old historic site _____ destroyed.

Unit 12 • You never know … 79

Vocabulary
bring and *take*, *come* and *go*

1 Complete the phrases with *bring*, *take*, *come* or *go*.

1 _____ ← a long time / a seat / a break

2 _____ ← people together / peace in the world / a souvenir back from holiday

3 _____ ← true / first in the race / to an end

4 _____ ← crazy / well together / wrong

2 Use the phrases from **1** to complete the sentences. Write the verbs in the correct tense.

1 When you go to Holland, could you **bring** me **back** some cheese?
2 I'm so proud of Ava – she _____ at school sports day.
3 Noah's dream _____ – he got a puppy for his eighth birthday.
4 Storytelling is a great way to _____.
5 Evelyn needs to _____ from work for a while. She's exhausted!
6 Please _____. The doctor will be with you in a minute.
7 I overslept this morning, I missed my train, then I lost £20 – what else can _____!
8 Wine and cheese _____.

Prepositions

3 EXTENSION Underline the correct preposition.

Verb + preposition
1 I'll pay *on / at / for* the coffees. You bought lunch.
2 I agree *on / at / with* you about most things, but not politics.
3 I'm thinking *of / on / for* living in France for a year.
4 I'm looking *at / on / for* Keri – have you seen her?
5 Can I talk *at / to / on* you for a moment?

Preposition + noun
1 I always get to work *by / on / at* time. I'm never late.
2 What's *at / in / on* TV tonight?
3 My flat is *at / in / on* the fifth floor.
4 I'm sorry. I opened your letter *for / by / in* accident.
5 I'm a bit busy *in / for / at* the moment. Can you call back later?

Adjective + preposition
1 We're so excited *about / with / of* our holiday. We're going to Greece next month.
2 Are you interested *of / about / in* photography?
3 Where have you been? I've been so worried *for / of / about* you!
4 I'm so proud *of / for / about* my son. He's studying to be a teacher.
5 I'm really angry *with / of / for* you! Why didn't you call or text me?

Noun + preposition
1 Congratulations *on / in / about* your exam results! You must be delighted!
2 Can I have a word *about / with / for* you for a minute?
3 We've got an invitation *with / in / to* Pauline's wedding, but we're away.
4 Would you like to see a photo *with / about / of* my children?
5 The advantage *for / of / about* living in a town is that everything is nearby.

Everyday English
Thank you and goodbye!

Add the missing words to complete the conversations.

1 **A** Bye Claude. I hope you have a *safe* journey. Who's picking you *up*?
  B My brother, Anton.

2 **A** Thank you so much a lovely evening. The food was delicious.
  B It was my pleasure. I'm you enjoyed it.

3 **A** Thanks for me. I've had a lovely few days.
  B It's been a. You know you're always to stay.
  A You're kind.

4 **A** Have a good and text me when you get home.
  B Will. Thanks for driving me to the airport.
  A No problem. Please my love to your parents.

🔊 **12.2** Listen and check.

📲 Go online for more skills and language practice.

REVIEW

16-year-old **Amber** is going on a French exchange, and her father is saying goodbye to her. Write the correct form of the verbs in brackets.

D Bye, honey! Have a really good time. If I ¹ *was/were* (be) 16 again, and going to Paris, I ² _____ (be) so excited.

A Bye, Dad. I *am* excited. I ³ _____ (text) you and Mum when I ⁴ _____ (arrive).

D I hope the Durands are a nice family. If you ⁵ _____ (not be) happy, you'll call us, won't you?

A Dad, don't worry. If I ⁶ _____ (not know) the family, I'd be nervous, but we all thought their daughter Celine was lovely when she stayed with us last year, didn't we? I'm sure her parents are lovely, too. If I ⁷ _____ (not like) them, or if anything goes wrong, I ⁸ _____ (let) you know.

D I know, I just worry. If something ⁹ _____ (happen) to you, I'd never forgive myself. Do you know what time you'll get there?

A If my plane ¹⁰ _____ (land) on time, I'll be at the Durand's apartment at about 8.00 this evening.

D OK. Have a safe journey. If you let me know when your flight home is, I ¹¹ _____ (pick) you up at the airport with a huge *Welcome home!* poster.

A Don't you dare, Dad! If you ¹² _____ (do) that, I'll walk straight past you! Just have a nice quiet time while I'm away!

🔊 **12.3** Listen and check.

📲 Go online to Check your progress.

Unit 12 • You never know … 81

Stop and check Units 9–12

Grammar

1 Choose the correct answer.

1 One day while she _____ flowers in the wood, she met a wolf.
 a was picking
 b picked
 c had picked
2 I knew that I _____ her somewhere before.
 a was meeting
 b 've met
 c 'd met
3 They promised to text _____ they arrived home.
 a as
 b as soon as
 c while
4 She _____ reply to her emails until after the holiday.
 a hasn't
 b didn't
 c hadn't
5 Why _____ me that you'd seen the film already?
 a haven't you told
 b hadn't you told
 c didn't you tell
6 The police said that they _____ the thief.
 a did catch
 b had caught
 c was caught
7 We went for a long walk, _____ it was raining hard.
 a although
 b however
 c after
8 The first text message _____ in 1989.
 a has been sent
 b was sent
 c had sent
9 Why _____ you invited to the party? Does Pam not like you?
 a were
 b weren't
 c haven't
10 How many bottles of champagne _____ at the wedding?
 a have been drunk
 b were drank
 c were drunk
11 They _____ together since they were at school.
 a 're going out
 b were going out
 c 've been going out
12 How long _____ to pass your driving test?
 a are you trying
 b have you been trying
 c have you tried
13 How many times _____ your driving test?
 a were you failed
 b have you been failing
 c have you failed
14 Oh no! I _____ mum's favourite vase!
 a broke
 b 've broken
 c 've been breaking
15 You'll be in big trouble when mum _____!
 a finds out
 b will find out
 c would find out
16 If I _____ a free weekend, I'll take you for a drive.
 a have
 b will have
 c 'd have
17 I'd buy a new car if I _____ the money.
 a would have
 b have
 c had
18 Careful! If you _____ where you are going, you'll fall!
 a look
 b don't look
 c won't look
19 We _____ go on holiday in June. We're not sure yet.
 a might
 b will
 c won't
20 If you tell me, I promise I _____ tell anyone else.
 a will
 b won't
 c wouldn't

SCORE   20

Vocabulary

2 Use the clues to complete the crossword.

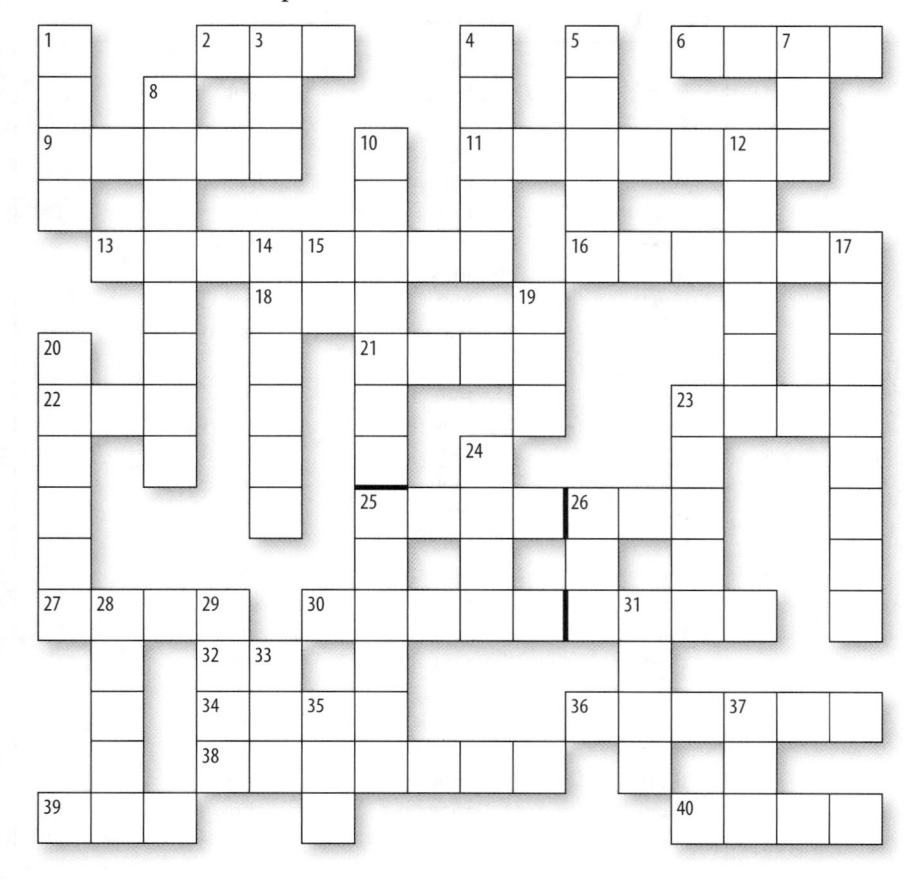

ACROSS

2. I came to England four years _____. (3)
6. This office is great – it's very _____-equipped. (4)
9. Our wedding day was a disaster – everything went _____! (5)
11. I don't want to be in the house, I want to go _____. (7)
13. The thing that you type on – or play! (8)
16. Thank you for _____ me – I've really enjoyed my stay. (6)
18. After a rest, we set _____ walking again. (3)
21. I had to pay a £100 _____ for parking there. (4)
22. With Netflix, you can watch a whole drama series in _____ go! (3)
23. If I had more _____ time, I'd take up painting. (4)
25. I often _____ _____ recipes in this cookbook. (4, 3)
27. At the school reunion Dan and I didn't recognize _____ other! (4)
30. I like your suggestions – I _____ _____ them all. (5,4)
32. We've run out _____ milk – can you buy some later? (2)
34. We _____ Grandma last week, sadly. She'd been ill for a long time. (4)
36. With good Wi-fi you can _____ films to your TV. (6)
38. Heidi has some lovely clothes – she's always well-_____. (7)
39. The hungry wolf _____ every last bit of Bertha. (3)
40. I might go out later, or I might _____ in. (4)

DOWN

1. I'm very tired. I think I'll lie _____ for a bit. (4)
3. My band are playing a _____ in the town hall tonight. (3)
4. We're very _____ of our daughter's success. (5)
5. Have you got a _____ to light the fire? (5)
7. That's not true! It's a _____! (3)
8. I think blue and green can go well _____. (8)
10. Those _____ _____ were red – why did you drive through them? (7,6)
12. The taxi _____ asked me which football team I support. (6)
14. 40% of video games are _____ by women. (6)
15. *Bubble Ball* can be used by children _____ all abilities. (2)
17. Carla will pay for the meal tonight – she's very _____. (8)
19. I don't have an answer right now. Can I _____ back to you later? (3)
20. I think it's time for a _____ break – I need an espresso! (6)
23. The _____ real paper was invented in China. (5)
24. Pat and Erin aren't here – they've _____ to London for the day. (4)
26. Many people play Tetris, but only a _____ master it. (3)
28. I'm really excited _____ the concert tomorrow! (5)
31. The book *Finding Gobi* might be made _____ a movie. (4)
33. Where have you been?! I've been waiting here _____ ages! (3)
35. I watched the whole box _____ of *The Crown* over the weekend! (3)
37. If you _____ more fresh food, you'll feel healthier. (3)

SCORE 40

TOTAL 60

Irregular verbs

Base form	Past Simple	Past participle
be	was/were	been
beat	beat	beaten
become	became	become
begin	began	begun
bend	bent	bent
bite	bit	bitten
blow	blew	blown
break	broke	broken
bring	brought	brought
build	built	built
buy	bought	bought
can	could	been able
catch	caught	caught
choose	chose	chosen
come	came	come
cost	cost	cost
cut	cut	cut
dig	dug	dug
do	did	done
draw	drew	drawn
dream	dreamed/dreamt	dreamed/dreamt
drink	drank	drunk
drive	drove	driven
eat	ate	eaten
fall	fell	fallen
feed	fed	fed
feel	felt	felt
fight	fought	fought
find	found	found
fit	fit	fit
fly	flew	flown
forget	forgot	forgotten
forgive	forgave	forgiven
freeze	froze	frozen
get	got	got
give	gave	given
go	went	been/gone
grow	grew	grown
hang	hung	hung
have	had	had
hear	heard	heard
hide	hid	hidden
hit	hit	hit
hold	held	held
hurt	hurt	hurt
keep	kept	kept
kneel	knelt	knelt
know	knew	known
lay	laid	laid
lead	led	led
learn	learned/learnt	learned/learnt
leave	left	left
lend	lent	lent
let	let	let
lie	lay	lain
light	lighted/lit	lighted/lit
lose	lost	lost
make	made	made
mean	meant	meant
meet	met	met
must	had to	had to
pay	paid	paid
put	put	put
read /riːd/	read /red/	read /red/
ride	rode	ridden
ring	rang	rung
rise	rose	risen
run	ran	run
say	said	said
see	saw	seen
sell	sold	sold
send	sent	sent
set	set	set
shake	shook	shaken
shine	shone	shone
shoot	shot	shot
show	showed	shown
shut	shut	shut
sing	sang	sung
sink	sank	sunk
sit	sat	sat
sleep	slept	slept
slide	slid	slid
speak	spoke	spoken
spend	spent	spent
spoil	spoiled/spoilt	spoiled/spoilt
spread	spread	spread
stand	stood	stood
steal	stole	stolen
stick	stuck	stuck
swim	swam	swum
take	took	taken
teach	taught	taught
tear	tore	torn
tell	told	told
think	thought	thought
throw	threw	thrown
understand	understood	understood
wake	woke	woken
wear	wore	worn
win	won	won
write	wrote	written

Phonetic symbols

Consonants

1	/p/	as in	**pen** /pen/
2	/b/	as in	**big** /bɪg/
3	/t/	as in	**tea** /tiː/
4	/d/	as in	**do** /duː/
5	/k/	as in	**cat** /kæt/
6	/g/	as in	**go** /gəʊ/
7	/f/	as in	**four** /fɔː/
8	/v/	as in	**very** /ˈveri/
9	/s/	as in	**son** /sʌn/
10	/z/	as in	**zoo** /zuː/
11	/l/	as in	**live** /lɪv/
12	/m/	as in	**my** /maɪ/
13	/n/	as in	**near** /nɪə/
14	/h/	as in	**happy** /ˈhæpi/
15	/r/	as in	**red** /red/
16	/j/	as in	**yes** /jes/
17	/w/	as in	**want** /wɒnt/
18	/θ/	as in	**thanks** /θæŋks/
19	/ð/	as in	**the** /ðə/
20	/ʃ/	as in	**she** /ʃiː/
21	/ʒ/	as in	**television** /ˈtelɪvɪʒn/
22	/tʃ/	as in	**child** /tʃaɪld/
23	/dʒ/	as in	**German** /ˈdʒɜːmən/
24	/ŋ/	as in	**English** /ˈɪŋglɪʃ/

Vowels

25	/iː/	as in	**see** /siː/
26	/ɪ/	as in	**his** /hɪz/
27	/i/	as in	**twenty** /ˈtwenti/
28	/e/	as in	**ten** /ten/
29	/æ/	as in	**stamp** /stæmp/
30	/ɑː/	as in	**father** /ˈfɑːðə/
31	/ɒ/	as in	**hot** /hɒt/
32	/ɔː/	as in	**morning** /ˈmɔːnɪŋ/
33	/ʊ/	as in	**football** /ˈfʊtbɔːl/
34	/uː/	as in	**you** /juː/
35	/ʌ/	as in	**sun** /sʌn/
36	/ɜː/	as in	**learn** /lɜːn/
37	/ə/	as in	**letter** /ˈletə/

Diphthongs (two vowels together)

38	/eɪ/	as in	**name** /neɪm/
39	/əʊ/	as in	**no** /nəʊ/
40	/aɪ/	as in	**my** /maɪ/
41	/aʊ/	as in	**how** /haʊ/
42	/ɔɪ/	as in	**boy** /bɔɪ/
43	/ɪə/	as in	**hear** /hɪə/
44	/eə/	as in	**where** /weə/
45	/ʊə/	as in	**tour** /tʊə/

> # OXFORD
> UNIVERSITY PRESS

Great Clarendon Street, Oxford, OX2 6DP, United Kingdom

Oxford University Press is a department of the University of Oxford.
It furthers the University's objective of excellence in research, scholarship,
and education by publishing worldwide. Oxford is a registered trade
mark of Oxford University Press in the UK and in certain other countries

© Oxford University Press 2019

The moral rights of the author have been asserted

First published in 2019

2023 2022
10 9 8 7 6

No unauthorized photocopying

All rights reserved. No part of this publication may be reproduced, stored
in a retrieval system, or transmitted, in any form or by any means, without
the prior permission in writing of Oxford University Press, or as expressly
permitted by law, by licence or under terms agreed with the appropriate
reprographics rights organization. Enquiries concerning reproduction outside
the scope of the above should be sent to the ELT Rights Department, Oxford
University Press, at the address above

You must not circulate this work in any other form and you must impose
this same condition on any acquirer

Links to third party websites are provided by Oxford in good faith and for
information only. Oxford disclaims any responsibility for the materials
contained in any third party website referenced in this work

ISBN: 978 0 19 452913 6

Printed in China

This book is printed on paper from certified and well-managed sources

ACKNOWLEDGEMENTS

Back cover photograph: Oxford University Press building/David Fisher

Cover Image: Getty Images (man on bicycle/Philipp Nemenz), (defocused street people/yavuzsariyildiz).

Illustrations by: Fausto Bianchi/Beehive Illustration p.58; Emma Brownjohn/New Division p.25; Simon Cooper p.7; Lucy Davey/The Artworks p.26; Guev pp.13 (Billy's room), 19, 36; John Haslam pp.10, 22, 48, 68, 70; Joanna Kerr/New Division p.18, 28, 79; Vince Reid/The Organisation pp.13 (men in café), 33, 52, 55; Mark Ruffle p.74; Amit Tayal/Beehive illustration p.59.

The publisher would like to thank the following for permission to reproduce photographs: 123RF pp.14 (James/Wavebreak Media Ltd), 15 (Snowdonia/Ollirg, Sheepdog/Eric Isselee), 16 (phone/Andriano), 24 (coffee beans/Anatolii Riepin), 29 (cheesecake/Tatiana Bralnina, coffee/Belchonock), 32 (Maddie/Lopolo, plane/Gino Santa Maria), 34 (bus stop/Andriy Popov, estate agent and couple/Kurhan), 44 (Brazil aerial view/Marchello74), 68 (headlights/Stillfx); The Australian War Memorial p.21 (medals); Alamy Images pp.6 (Garlen/MORISSE Périg), 18 (Ireland landscape/robertharding, King of Tory Island/Hemis), 21 (Nancy Wake/UtCon Collection), 24 (newspapers/Alan Wilson), 33 (RosaIreneBetancourt 12), 34 (Japanese app/NicoElNino), 37 (boy driving/headshot of boy/Drive Images), 41 (Koch brewery/US Labor Department), 49 (Xinhua), 60 (Oskana Kuzmina), 62 (dancer/Mihai Blanaru), 64 (Juan Carlos Baena), 67 (Egyptian papyrus/ART Collection), 70 (Primo Dul Ravel), 74 (pregnant couple/Juice Images), 76 (ship/imageBROKER, manta ray/Carlos Villoch-MagicSea.com), 77 (Land Rover/Wayne Hutchinson), 81 (dad and daughter hug/Westend61 GmbH); Getty Images pp.9 (Menna and Jen/Chung Sung-Jun, skiing/Lintao Zhang/Getty Sport), 12 (Jacob Niblett/Contour), 20 (man and dog in car/Shelley Wood/The Image Bank), 41 (lager label/Bloomberg), 43 (Neal Haynes/Contour), 47 (Malavath Poorna in t shirt/Prakash Mathema/Stringer), 50 (boxer/Colin Anderson/Blend Images), 51 (older man talking/Westend61, boxer/Fox Images/Hulton Archive), 63 (Todor Tsvetkov/E+), 69 (Bubble Ball/Bloomberg), 76 (shark/ullstein bild), 79 (volcano/Tom Pfeiffer/Photographer's Choice); iStock pp.6, (Johanna/People Images, Anna and Don/michaeljung), 8 (bowdenimages), 14 (Serena/Steve Debenport), 15 (Owen/Pidjoe), 16 (barbeque/Martin-dm), 17 (couple/Xavier Arnau), 23 (Margot/drbimages), 34 (starting line athletes/FatCamera/Vetta), 46 (me/Kali9, Samantha/Drazen_, Jenny/Henry/m-imagephotography, Chris/Kate_sept2004), 62 (scrabble letters/Mattjeacock, man and fan/Mediaphotos), 65 (hummus/Alleko, seatbelt/Andresr), 66 (DieterMeyr), 74 (showing off ring/Steve Devenport, gravestone/Ajkkafe), 77 (cottage/Nikada, painting/Vladimir Vladimirov), 78 (Siphotograhy), 79 (Yellowstone/Dszc); NASA p.20 (Cassini); The Observer p.35 (Mohammad Razai/Karen Robinson); Robert Nay p.69 (Robert Nay); Oxford University Press pp.18 (backpack/Shutterstock), 20 (umbrella), 24 (bar chocolate/ice cream cone/cupcake/Shutterstock), 27 (fish and chips/Shutterstock), 47 (Mount Everest/Shutterstock); Rex Shutterstock pp.18 (Tony Hawkes), 20 (Fauja Singh/Keystone US-ZUMA), 21 (soldiers/Victor Console/Daily Mail), 47 (Malavath Poorna receives award/STR/Epa), 61 (Dion Leonard and Gobi/Matteo Bazzi/EPA-EFE), 73 (Elvis Presley/Granger, Marilyn Monroe/Moviestore Collection); Shutterstock pp.11 (SpeedKingz), 15 (retriever dog/Africa Studio), 16 (trainers/Robyn Mackenzie), 18 (signpost/Pincasso, fridge/Vorm in Bleed), 22 (exercising man/Sebastian Gauert), 23 (handbag/tale, cupcake/Ruth Black), 24 (chocolates/Jiri Hera, cup of coffee/YKTR, glass bowl/urfin, wine glass/Mariyana M, white paper/Suradech Prapairat, ice cream tubs/Ffolas, raspberry cake/Elena Shashkina), 27 (fish and chip shop/Travellight, Harry Ramsdens sign/Roger Utting), 28 (pineapple/Valentina Proskurina, cauliflower/Egor Rodynchenko, courgette/melon/Akepong srichaichana), 29 (potatoes/I T A L O), 32 (tornado/Solarseven, Dermot/Goodluz), 34 (couple and fridge/Iakov Filimonov), 35 (Cambridge/Evikka), 38 (Sabine/Monkey Business Images, Great Wall of China/Aphotostory), 40 (Estrada Anton), 42 (Africa Studio), 44 (friends/Filipe Frazao, Copacabana beach/Aleksandar Todorovic), 45 (Rita/Jaco/Dean Drobot), 48 (Andrey_Popov), 50 (chef/Wavebreakmedia), 53 (Tyler Olson), 54 (bite apple/Michelangeloop, smell flowers/Rafal Olechowski, feet walk/Morakot Kawinchan, hands clap/Emily Frost, ear/Brian A Jackson, fingers type/NA image), 62 (brown bear/Martin Mecnarowski, person at window/Africa Studio, football match/Paolo Bona, matchstick/Peter Janco, witch/Irina Alexandrovna), 65 (World Cup/fifg), 67 (recycling/Petovarga), 68 (headache/g-stockstudio, headphones/All for you friend), 72 (ChickenStock images), 73 (locks of hair/Makovsky Art, Justin Bieber/s_bukley), 74 (women talking/Milles Studio, man with flu/Africa Studio, mum and baby/ChameleonsEye), 75 (magicinfoto), 77 (Paula/g-stockstudio, beach/Maxim Tupikov, dog/rebeccaashworth, vegetable garden/Sirtravelalot), 80 (goir), 81 (man waving/Prasit Rodphan); Thomas Nelson p.61 (Cover of Finding Gobi by Dion Leonard (2018).

The authors and publisher are grateful to those who have given permission to reproduce the following extracts and adaptations of copyright material: p.35 'The refugee from Afghanistan'. Reproduced by permission of Mohammad Razai. p.77 Fictitious interview with Juliette Binoche. Reproduced by permission of INTERTALENT on behalf of Juliette Binoche.

Sources: p.9 www.mennaandjen.co.uk, p.69 www.money.cnn.com